T0329027

CAMBRIDGE LIBRARY COLLECTION

Books of enduring scholarly value

Music

The systematic academic study of music gave rise to works of description, analysis and criticism, by composers and performers, philosophers and anthropologists, historians and teachers, and by a new kind of scholar - the musicologist. This series makes available a range of significant works encompassing all aspects of the developing discipline.

Letters of Richard Wagner to Emil Heckel

A great admirer of Richard Wagner, the music publisher Emil Heckel (1831–1908) founded the first Wagner Society in Mannheim in 1871. His purpose was to inspire others to help raise the necessary funds for the inaugural Bayreuth Festival. William Ashton Ellis (1852–1919) abandoned his medical career in order to devote himself to his Wagner studies. Best known for his translations of Wagner's prose works, he published in 1899 this English translation of Heckel's memoirs (originally edited by his son Karl), interwoven with letters from Wagner to Heckel, who is described by the composer as his 'energetic friend'. Notwithstanding the stylistic idiosyncrasies of the translation, the work provides a valuable first-hand account of the progress made towards establishing what would become one of the world's most prestigious music festivals. The letters span the years 1871 to 1883.

Cambridge University Press has long been a pioneer in the reissuing of out-of-print titles from its own backlist, producing digital reprints of books that are still sought after by scholars and students but could not be reprinted economically using traditional technology. The Cambridge Library Collection extends this activity to a wider range of books which are still of importance to researchers and professionals, either for the source material they contain, or as landmarks in the history of their academic discipline.

Drawing from the world-renowned collections in the Cambridge University Library and other partner libraries, and guided by the advice of experts in each subject area, Cambridge University Press is using state-of-the-art scanning machines in its own Printing House to capture the content of each book selected for inclusion. The files are processed to give a consistently clear, crisp image, and the books finished to the high quality standard for which the Press is recognised around the world. The latest print-on-demand technology ensures that the books will remain available indefinitely, and that orders for single or multiple copies can quickly be supplied.

The Cambridge Library Collection brings back to life books of enduring scholarly value (including out-of-copyright works originally issued by other publishers) across a wide range of disciplines in the humanities and social sciences and in science and technology.

Letters of Richard Wagner to Emil Heckel

With a Brief History of the Bayreuth Festivals

EDITED BY KARL HECKEL
TRANSLATED BY WILLIAM ASHTON ELLIS

CAMBRIDGE
UNIVERSITY PRESS

University Printing House, Cambridge, CB2 8BS, United Kingdom

Cambridge University Press is part of the University of Cambridge.
It furthers the University's mission by disseminating knowledge in the pursuit of
education, learning and research at the highest international levels of excellence.

www.cambridge.org
Information on this title: www.cambridge.org/9781108078597

© in this compilation Cambridge University Press 2015

This edition first published 1899
This digitally printed version 2015

ISBN 978-1-108-07859-7 Paperback

This book reproduces the text of the original edition. The content and language reflect
the beliefs, practices and terminology of their time, and have not been updated.

Cambridge University Press wishes to make clear that the book, unless originally published
by Cambridge, is not being republished by, in association or collaboration with,
or with the endorsement or approval of, the original publisher or its successors in title.

Wagner
Letters to Heckel

RICHARD WAGNER'S PROSE WORKS

Translated by

Wm. Ashton Ellis.

Complete in eight volumes, Demy 8vo, at
12s. 6d. net each.

*** Seven volumes of the English translation are
already published :—

The remaining volume to be issued before the end
of 1899.

Kegan Paul, Trench, Trübner and Co., London.

———

The Perfect Wagnerite, a Commentary on the
Ring of the Niblung.   By Bernard Shaw.   Fcap.
8vo.   3s. 6d.

Grant Richards, 9 Henrietta St., Covent Garden,
London, W.C.

LETTERS OF RICHARD
WAGNER TO EMIL HEC-
KEL: WITH A BRIEF HIS-
TORY OF THE BAYREUTH
FESTIVALS. TRANSLAT-
ED AND INDEXED BY
WM. ASHTON ELLIS.

London: Grant Richards, 9
Henrietta St. Covent Garden,
London, W.C. 1899.

Preface

[*I* SHALL *not delay the reader of this fascinating little book for any longer than it will take him—and, I may hope, also her—to note the following three facts: 1st that Herr Emil Heckel, still a member of the Bayreuth Council of Administration—or " Verwaltungsrath"—was founder of the very earliest Wagner Society, and has ever been one of the staunchest and most unselfish friends of the Bayreuth cause; 2nd that Frau Wagner has kindly given her express authority and sanction to my translating these letters of her husband's; 3rd that Herr Karl Heckel, editor of the German book, has most generously granted me the exclusive right of rendering his father's recollections into English, subject to the sole condition that their rendering shall be faithful: my own contribution to the book is therefore limited to the very few notes which bear the symbol " Tr."—June* 1899, *W.A.E.*]

By invitation of the editor of the *Neue Deutsche*

Rundschau my father last year jotted down his reminiscences of Richard Wagner. Shortly afterwards Frau Wagner gave her most gracious consent to the publication of all the master's letters to my father. The next step, therefore, obviously was to publish both reminiscences and letters in one and the same volume. I undertook their combination.

In order to weld the two into one whole, a complete remodelling of the "reminiscences" was unavoidable. Their subjective character has been preserved, however, even where it was tinged with a certain polemical colour from the days of war.

As to Wagner's letters themselves, in very few cases has it been requisite to make omissions. These are scrupulously indicated in the text.

Since, according to Bismarck's epigram, the publication of private letters almost always "sets their author in his shirt-sleeves on the balcony," many a circumstantial explanation of minor points has become necessary, not to give spiteful neighbours too many opportunities for "misconstruction." The reproducing of such details undoubtedly thrusts the narrator more into the foreground than he himself could wish ; yet, in a book of memoirs, that danger is not easy to avoid. Does it really need apology?

Surely not, if I cite the original title of these recollections : "*In the service of Art.*" For that denotes the sense in which to take the record of many memories of personal intercourse with the master, as also his recognition of the steadfastness of his "Strategos" in the Bayreuth work.

THE EDITOR [Karl Heckel].

MANNHEIM, 1st *January* 1898.

In the year 1853, at the age of two-and-twenty, I heard the *Tannhäuser*-overture for the first time, conducted by Liszt at Carlsruhe. I was filled with rage at this "horrible" music, which flatly contradicted all my previous notions of the "beautiful." I gave my wrath as free a rein, as my companion H. M. Schletterer—thereafter a well-known opponent of Wagner's—gave his immoderate enthusiasm. Not for some time was I afforded occasion to change my mind; for the new art was not then practised in my native city, Mannheim. Our Court-conductor, Vincenz Lachner, was its determined and powerful adversary. To be sure, he was compelled to put on *Tannhäuser*, and later *Lohengrin*; but the solecisms of the production were little calculated to recruit for Wagner.

Ten years after that concert, and again at Carlsruhe, I heard the "Walküren-Ritt" conducted by Wagner himself. This time I underwent a strong impression, and was convinced that similar concerts, personally conducted by Wagner, would break the ice at Mannheim too. I had some desire to bring this about, but my zeal was not yet warm enough to urge me to active measures.   However, the longing remained, to make the acquaintance of a Wagnerian stage-work in model rendering.

At Venice, on my way home from Italy with my wife in the summer of 1868, I read the announcement of the *first* performance of *Die Meistersinger von Nürnberg* at Munich.   My decision was swiftly taken : off to Munich.

This perfect and complete production under Wagner's personal superintendence, with Hans von Bülow as conductor and Hans Richter as leader on the stage, had the effect upon me of a revelation— and shewed me the task of my life.

Arrived home at Mannheim, I induced my father, as President of the Committee of Management of the Court-theatre, to have the *Meistersinger* mounted. A battle royal ensued with Lachner, who, unable to prevent the performance itself, made cuts in the score amounting to 171 lines of verse in the first act, 137 in the second, and 345 in the third ; among them, all but the opening words of Sachs' monologue, and the chorus " Wach' auf ! "   Nevertheless the thing was a success.

Next year I got a " Concert-union " founded, for the financial support of things musical.   Though there could be no question of informing it with a definite tendence, I hoped to have won at least a basis for the reform of musical matters ; and I drafted a letter to Wagner, inviting him to conduct a concert in person.   My enthusiasm, however, was

in advance of the times. There was no chance of
my plan being adopted, and the letter had to stay
unsent.

At that time, even among the friends of the *new
art*, in most respectable circles there reigned a secret
dread of confessing oneself a Wagnerian. The
calumniations of his person and distortions of his
object, that crowded to the light on every hand, cast
their reflection on his adherents also, to the detriment
of their position in civic life. Only slowly did there
form a small community of unscared advocates. On
the 30th April 1871 these made their first public appearance in the music-room of my pianoforte-ware-
house, where they rendered Wagner's *Kaisermarsch* on
two concert-grands a few weeks after its composition. The performance was undertaken by Herr A.
Hänlein, Dr. Zeroni, Herr Ernst Bassermann and
Herr Rud. Artaria, conducted by Herr Ferd.Langer.
Members of the Court-theatre and two or three vocal
unions sang the closing chorus. For a repetition
the doors and windows were thrown open; our
enthusiasm spread to those outside, and, at a time
so strung to patriotism, the whole street took up the
final chant.

The first performance of the *Kaisermarsch* had
taken place on April 14, 1871, in Berlin, under
Bilse, followed by Gungl on April 23 at Leipzig.
On May the fifth it was played in Berlin under
Wagner himself, for the benefit of the "Kaiser-
Wilhelm-Stiftung."

The restoration of the German Reich strengthened

Wagner's belief in the development of a truly German Art and Culture. Inspired by this confidence, he issued a public appeal, under the title "Ueber die Aufführung des Bühnenfestspieles : Der Ring des Nibelungen," in which he begged the friends of his art simply to make themselves known to him by name. In answer to this appeal I (alas! alone) wrote the master as a personal stranger on May 15, 1871, that he might count myself with the friends of his art, asking him to tell me what they first could do to contribute to the success of his great national enterprise.

After a day or two, Wagner's answer arrived :—

Dear Sir,
    Heartily thanking you for your proofs of friendship, I have above all to acknowledge the value of your announcement that you wish to share in the facilitation of my great undertaking. For further particulars I beg you kindly to address yourself to Herr K. Tausig, 35 Dessauer Strasse, Berlin. Until a Patronat-Committee shall have been constituted, he has provisionally taken over the business side of the matter, and will give you precise information as to the mode in which your sympathy may be made effectual.
                With every compliment,
                    Yours faithfully
                        RICHARD WAGNER.

LUCERNE, 19th May, 1871.

Instead of writing, I made a personal journey to Tausig, and learnt from him the plan for raising the requisite funds through the issue of a thousand *Patronat-vouchers* at three-hundred thalers [about

£45] apiece. My proposal to found " Wagner-
Vereins," to enable the less affluent to share in
taking up these vouchers, met his approval.

Returned to Mannheim, I at once began to found
the Verein. Its origin and evolution are described
at length in a book of my son's.[1]

Despatching the statutes to Tausig, I asked him
if it would be at all possible to induce Wagner to
conduct a concert at Mannheim himself. At like
time I informed Tausig of my intention to urge the
foundation of Wagner-societies in other towns. He
answered me :—

Dear Sir,
Your " Wagner-Verein " is an excellent idea, and,
with such earnest and persistent advocacy, the result cannot
but be gratifying. I will write Wagner about the conducting of a concert at Mannheim, but scarcely think he
will decide on such another trip. The inner circle of the
Patronat consists, as I told you before, of Fr. Liszt, Madame
von Muchanoff, Baroness von Schleinitz, and myself; the
full Committee list cannot be issued for a few months to
come.
So soon as I receive a favourable answer from Wagner,
I will drop you a line. The signed applications for
Patronat-vouchers please send to me at Berlin.
Yours very truly
CARL TAUSIG.

WEIMAR, 7th June, 1871.

Dear Sir,
I can see no objection to your plans for a " Wagner-
Verein," excepting that we shall encounter difficulties and

[1] Karl Heckel, " Die Bühnenfestspiele in Bayreuth " Authentischer Beitrag
zur Geschichte ihrer Enstehung und Entwickelung. (E. W. Fritzsch, Leipzig.)

delays in cashing the Patronat subscriptions. As the theatre, i.e. the building and other preliminaries, will be taken in hand by the end of this autumn, we shall soon require to have the disposal of substantial means.—At any other time Herr Wagner would have accepted your invitation to conduct a concert at Mannheim ; but the composition of the Nibelungen forbids him to split up his energy in any way that parts him from his work.

With best compliments,
Yours faithfully,
CARL TAUSIG.

BERLIN, 17*th June*, 1871.

Regarding the concert, a more favourable prospect was opened up by a letter of Wagner's, after I had acquainted him with the satisfactory progress of the Verein :—

Dear Sir,
    Delighted by your acceptable news, I confine myself at present to answering the wish you have expressed to me. I am quite certain that it would offer a most agreeable diversion to my very secluded life, to take a few days' outing to conduct such a species of concert among friends. Only, for the moment I should not care to pledge myself to any given date, as—after many outward exertions—I have only just arrived at settling down to my work. Rely on it, however, that I will let you know in good time—probably in the autumn ; and I shall rely on you for its being something proper.

With sincerest compliments,
RICHARD WAGNER.

LUCERNE, 21*st June*, 1871.

By Tausig's sudden death on July 17, 1871, Wagner lost one of the ablest and most provident of his adherents. Tausig had intended to form an orchestra in Berlin expressly to perform appropriate portions of the *Ring des Nibelungen* in the concert-room. This project had a twofold aim : to introduce the public to the work, and so to familiarise the executants with its style that they might form the nucleus of the future Bayreuth orchestra.

A few questions which I had addressed to Wagner, touching preparations for the Mannheim concert, were kindly answered by Frau Wagner. She had already apprised me by letter that Wagner, of course, declined any honorarium for the concert.

Honoured Sir,
    My husband again requests me to thank you most sincerely in his name ; your organisation of the Verein to him seems admirable, and he begs you will have the kindness to send him two more prospectuses, since he has already despatched the former two as models.

As regards the concert, he assumes that its interest will consist in his conducting it ; consequently he deems vocal numbers superfluous. The orchestra which you have specified is what he needs, and the programme will therefore be composed of a Beethoven symphony, the two marches (King and Kaiser), the Lohengrin or Tristan prelude, and the Tannhäuser-overture. A fortnight before the concert my husband will send you more exact particulars. Should not the Patronat-vouchers, to be acquired with the proceeds of the concert, be raffled for the benefit of the orchestra ? [1]

How would it be, honoured Sir, if you placed yourself in communication with other cities, so that the Wagner

---

[1] The members of the orchestra claimed no pay. On the other hand they took part in the ballot for Patronat-vouchers, as they had entered into full rights of membership of the union.

Verein might spread from Mannheim over Germany? I think it would be well if this business had its centre with you. If this is your view also, I only beg you to confirm it, and I would give you the addresses of persons in various towns to whom an appeal might be sent with certainty of good results.

To the most friendly greetings of my husband I add, most honoured Sir, the assurance of my own esteem.

COSIMA WAGNER
née Liszt.

TRIBSCHEN, NEAR LUCERNE, 16*th July*, 1871.

This letter was forwarded to me at Partenkirchen, whence I set out for Vienna, to co-operate with Dr. Kafka in founding a Verein on the spot.

In my answer to Frau Wagner I declared my readiness to undertake the central management of the Vereins. At like time I asked whether the visit of Herr Hänlein, committee-man of the Mannheim Verein, would be welcome at Tribschen for discussion of the concert preliminaries. This question was answered in a letter written by Frau Wagner at the master's dictation :—

TRIBSCHEN, NEAR LUCERNE, 12*th August*, 1871.

My dear Sir,
I shall be pleased to receive the pianist Herr Hänlein, and to give him the desired details of the concert.

I have written to Court-pianoforte-purveyor Karl Bechstein in Berlin, praying him to take Karl Tausig's place ;[1] until I receive his answer, communications may be sent to her Excellency Freifrau von Schleinitz, Ministry of the Royal and Imperial Household, Wilhelmstrasse, Berlin.—

[1] He declined.

No public appeal can be entertained by the Berlin committee, as its first principle has been to keep to personal and private paths. With best thanks and friendliest greeting,

RICHARD WAGNER.

Herr Hänlein was quite enthusiastic in the report of his interview with Wagner, who had often spoken "like a Seer"; he told me that Wagner meant to apply to the Grand Duke of Baden for the participation of the Carlsruhe orchestra in our concert.

To establish a common base of operations between the Vereins and the Patronat-committee, I addressed myself to Freifrau von Schleinitz, who was at all times most successfully at work in private for the undertaking.

SALZBURG, 17*th August*, 1871.

Dear Sir,
        Your lines of the 14th inst. have this moment reached me here at Salzburg.—I hasten to inform you that to-day we travel *via* Munich to Lucerne, from which place I will write you in full after I have had a talk with Wagner. —I have already written to Dr. Kafka in Vienna, telling him how glad I should be if you would submit to the labour of taking over the whole business department of the great undertaking, making the Verein founded by yourself at Mannheim its centre.—

With fervent wishes for the success of your efforts, I remain with high esteem

Yours faithfully,

Freifrau VON SCHLEINITZ.

At the beginning of September Baron von Loën,

General Intendant of the Weimar Court-theatre,
informed me that he had been entrusted with "the
supreme control of the Patronat," and that he
thought it necessary to form a "General Council"
consisting of himself and the heads of the various
local Wagner-Vereins, in order to issue a public
appeal to found additional unions.

I expressed my entire concurrence with this plan,
and begged Baron von Loën to carry out his intention as soon as possible, since several unions had
already been formed on the Mannheim model.   In
spite of further negotiations by letter and word
of mouth with Baron von Loën, who seemed to
regard his task too strictly in the light of a repre-
sentative, this "General Council" never came into
existence.

As it had been made known in the papers that
Wagner would conduct two concerts in Vienna, I
asked the master whether the Mannheim concert
might not also be announced.   Without his express
consent I would make nothing public, but attached
great weight to whatever seemed adapted to shew the
world that the enterprise was no longer in the clouds.
From the following two letters of the master's I first
learnt how onerous the preparations were to Wagner,
and for awhile avoided all importuning about the
concert.

My dear Sir,
        Forgive this delay with my answer.   Precisely in
the last few weeks I have been engaged in active corre-

spondence about the steps immediately necessary for my undertaking, which needs must suffer a considerable postponement if the first building - operations for the theatre cannot be begun this autumn. It is essential for me to know the present amount of subscriptions, to be able to judge whether I can give the needful orders to the architect and machinist; for, if the date announced by me is to be observed, the preliminary work must commence at once. I therefore beg you in particular to acquaint Herr von Loën as soon as possible with the results of your labours in Mannheim to date, so that he may be in the position to inform me of the grand total in good time.

In a favourable event I then propose to meet the architect and machinist at Bayreuth toward the end of this month, to settle all the requisites for the laying of the foundation-stone —to which, my dear Sir, I propose to invite yourself and the principal officers of the other Vereins. In every respect such a meeting, from which I should have to address a word to the public too, would help the progress of our enterprise; so that, even should delays arise thereafter, I eagerly desire the execution of my plan.—

I am sorry that a very premature announcement, that I intend giving concerts in Vienna, has somewhat upset you. Certainly, the rumour of my acceptance for Mannheim awoke in my Viennese friends a like wish for my personal intervention, and I could do no else than declare the same good-will to Vienna as to Mannheim. Now it is to be feared that every union in the various towns on whose co-operation I must count will advance a similar claim upon me, and the strength which I have promised to sacrifice in full to the execution of my work itself will be frittered away beforehand on amassing the material means, with incalculable consequences to myself. I undisguisedly acquaint you with this fear, without, however, withdrawing the promise I gave you: merely it would reassure me, if I could move you to a little patience, and if you would not be too pressing about the date of my concert-visit to Mannheim. To Vienna, also, I have only been able to give an indefinite consent as yet: I should much prefer our all assembling soon at Bayreuth, when this concert business also could be definitely arranged.

With the warmest acknowledgment of your most amiable services, and the request that you will present my best compliments to our valued friends in Mannheim,

I remain with all esteem
Yours faithfully
RICHARD WAGNER.

LUCERNE, 1st October, 1871.

Dear Herr Heckel,

Allow me, in the thick of business, to report you just one thing: namely, that according to the architect's latest statement the building of the theatre cannot be begun, and consequently the foundation-stone cannot be laid, before March. At the end of this month I shall go to Bayreuth, to clear up all anxieties about the plot of land etc. I believe, however, that a meeting of delegates from the Vereins would have no particular object before that desired occasion in March. Until then we shall probably have to see what each Verein is able to accomplish by itself. I still remain disposed to come to you and conduct a concert in the interim: further particulars I must reserve for a somewhat freer time than the present.

Heartiest greeting from
Yours faithfully
RICHARD WAGNER.

LUCERNE, 3rd November 1871.

A little earlier I had written Wagner: "I think the collecting of funds by the Vereins makes your brilliant undertaking a truly *national* one. How fine it would be, if the Vereins could be connected up—for which I strive with all my heart—so that, even after the first performances of your Bühnenfestspiel at Bayreuth, they might continue to aid your further labours at every season." Now that the meeting of delegates from the Vereins had been postponed, I myself sent Wagner a plan of organisation for a "German Wagner-Verein." Upon receipt of his answer I likewise sent the sketch of a "Call."

Dear Herr Heckel,
  Your proposal is firstrate : if such a unification comes to vigorous life, it will be the very thing I want. Meanwhile the strength of the situation still resides in its single robust parts. It is *units* that offer the most solid support at present. The society "Wagneriana" in Berlin lately voted the purchase of sixty (60) Patronat-vouchers, and the engagement of the whole orchestra. Vienna *promises* that it will shew itself equally generous in course of this winter. At Leipzig, on the other hand, $\frac{3}{4}$ of a voucher has been signed till now : in Munich—per Vereins—absolutely nothing, so far as I know. You in Mannheim alone have proved yourselves alive. Nevertheless, I comprehend that only by means of a large and general association, can the enterprise be lastingly and resultfully insured : therefore I think your proposals much more than simply worth consideration.

As to the date of my journey, at present I can say no more than that it will occur at latest in the first part of December, when I think of spending at least two days in Munich. At Bayreuth everything is already stirring in the most auspicious fashion ; my wishes are met with the most earnest attention. There I shall arrange whatever is needful, especially as concerns the site (which the town will probably present to me), so that the building may begin in March.   But where are the heads of Vereins, to be called thither (or to Leipzig—according to Herr von Loën)? Beyond your Mannheim Verein I know none that has done anything hitherto, or even made itself worth noticing, as a Verein.   Herr Dr. Kafka *will* shew us in time, with his Viennese, how things are going there.   So I think that a convocation would have no meaning before next March at Bayreuth.   For the moment the really important thing appears to me, that you should issue a strongly-worded appeal in the sense you have conveyed to me by your draft. By next March we should know the full extent of the response, and *then* a calling of the clans at Bayreuth (for the foundation-laying) would have some meaning.

I hope you are of my opinion ; and perhaps you will have the kindness to communicate your views to Herr von Loën, at like time giving him my best compliments.

With all respect, Yours faithfully
RICHARD WAGNER.

LUCERNE, *9th November*, 1871.

Dear Sir,

Herewith I return you your draft, which has my entire approval.   May the thing take its course, and the German shew that he understands at last to pay the needful tribute to such earnest and persistent efforts on behalf of so shamefully neglected, and withal so boundlessly influential a branch of public art, as that on which I have staked my life.   It is splendidly encouraging, my dear Herr Heckel, to light on people of your stamp.

Of the " green pamphlet "[1] on the Production of the Nibelungen-ring there still stand at your disposal, here as

---

[1] " Ueber die Aufführung des Bühnenfestspieles : der Ring des Nibelungen." Eine Mittheilung und Aufforderung an die Freunde seiner Kunst von Richard Wagner, Leipzig, Verlag von E. W. Fritzsch, 1871. [See *Richard Wagner's Prose Works*, vol. v., " Final Report, etc."—TR.]

well, a good number of copies for distribution. If you wish it, I will send you some.—

As regards all money matters, and so on, I beg you to treat with Herr v. Loën alone. The banker Cohn, however, has also undertaken to provide for interest on the incoming funds until they are required.

With all respect,
Yours faithfully
RICHARD WAGNER.

LUCERNE, 13th *November* 1871.

A report in a Darmstadt newspaper, that it was contemplated to hold the Bühnenfestspiels [Stage-festivals] in the Court-theatre there, made me telegraph to Wagner at Tribschen before issuing the said public Call. He answered by the same route :—

Darmstadt unknown. Town-councillor Bodmer's offer. All a misunderstanding. Bayreuth decision unalterable. Call can go out unhindered.

Wagner.

The " Call " signed by the Mannheim Wagner-Verein was issued forthwith. Circulated far and wide, partly through direct despatch, partly through reprint in German and foreign journals, it led to the formation of fresh Vereins.

In a letter to Wagner I enclosed my photograph, and touched once more on the concert business. I was highly delighted by his kind assent. The question, whether he proposed to obtain the co-operation of the Carlsruhe orchestra himself, he answered per telegram :—

Esteemed!   Have to do with you at Mannheim, with nobody at Carlsruhe.   Provision of means left entirely to you; answer only for my person.

Wagner.

The preparations for the concert necessitated various queries, answered in three more letters to myself.

Honoured Sir,
        To come at once to the point on which you probably are most intent, I take leave to inform you that from the evening of December 16 I stand at your disposal for a Mannheim concert, if so it must be (to gain a few extra 5 fl.[1] contributors!)

The rehearsals could take place on the 17th and 18th, the performance on the 19th or 20th.   As your room is small, I am afraid to introduce a chorus.   If a large hall (and consequently a *strong* chorus) were possible, I should propose to end the concert with "Wacht auf!" and the close from the Meistersinger: "Ehrt eure deutsche Meister"—with barytone solo (Hans Sachs).

Further 1. Overture to the Magic Flute (Mozart).
        2. Symphony in A-major (Beethoven).
        3. Prelude to Lohengrin.
        4. (Subject to that condition) the above-named fragments from the Meistersinger.   Preceding them: the Prelude to the Meistersinger.

The whole might begin with the Kaisermarsch.   I think that would be about enough music?—

Frau v. Muchanoff resides: Warsaw, Palais Potocki.—

Everything else is good and in order.   I stay here till December 7.— Best thanks for your photograph: at

---

[1] The subscription to the Mannheim Wagner-Verein was five guldens a member.

Mannheim they shall take my physiognomy too, to enable me to return the compliment.

With the most respectful greetings,
Yours sincerely
RICHARD WAGNER.

25th November, 1871.

My dear Sir,

There's to be a concert—consequently an end to tranquillity ! I knew it !—

Well, well !—

Your arrangements as regards the time and the rehearsals are excellent. The smallness of the place is bad : what do you mean by the " Theatersaal "[1] then ?

If there is really to be no chorus, I beg there may be no singing at all. We will wind up with the prelude and closing scene from Tristan und Isolde—instead of the closing scene from the Meistersinger. The parts for this please ask —in my name—from Kapellmeister C. Eckert in Berlin. They belong to *me*, and were merely lent to him.—

Accordingly the following programme : no division, but

As introduction : Prelude to Lohengrin.

1. Overture to the Magic Flute.
2. A-major Symphony.
3. Prelude to the Meistersinger.
4. Prelude and Close from Tristan und Isolde.
5. Kaisermarsch.

It doesn't look very grand, but will sound all right.—

In any case I should like you to reserve me six good seats.—

Could you also kindly take the trouble to find me good quarters ? As my wife is going to meet me at Mannheim,

---

[1] In my letter I had used this abbreviation for the concert-hall in the theatre-building.

C

accompanied by her eldest little daughter, I shall want, besides a sittingroom, two bedrooms with 3 beds.—

I congratulate you on the good reception of your Call by the newspapers. The [Augsburg] "Allgemeine," it is true, has uttered not a word as yet—presumably for cogent reasons.—

Greet our friends, and accept the very best thanks of
Yours sincerely
RICHARD WAGNER.

LUCERNE, 27*th November*, 1871.

*   *
*

18th December
Morning 1. (minor rehearsal).
Afternoon 2.   ditto.
19th December
Morning: supplementary rehearsal.
Evening: full rehearsal.
20th December. A little private entertainment for myself and a *very* few immediate friends, to play through a little private composition. A favour and special politeness to be asked of

6 to 8 first	}	violinists,	
7 to 8 second			
4	.	.	viola-players,
4	.	.	violoncellists,
2 to 3	.	contrabassists,	
1	.	.	flautist,
1	.	.	oboist,
2	.	.	clarinetists,
2	.	.	horn-players,
1	.	.	bassoon-player,
and 1	.	.	trumpeter.

The parts I will bring with me.

Get as much money out of the general rehearsal as you like. Not to trifle with the character of an artistic preparation, however, the preliminary rehearsals will be confined to ourselves.

These, my estimable Heckel, are about all the directions for which you asked me.

Should anything occur, I am in Munich from the 9th to the 12th (address: Franz Mrazeck, Wittelsbacher Platz No. 3), then at Bayreuth: [Hotel] Sonne.—

With cordial greetings,

Yours faithfully

RICHARD WAGNER.

LUCERNE, 6th December, 1871.

1 foot	Trombones	Drums	Percussion
1½ ft.	Horns	Trumpets	Bassoons
2⅓ ft. raised	Oboes	Flutes	Clarinets

ORCHESTRA.

These letters were followed by a few telegrams, among them the following:

Programme misintelligible. Please, introduction Kaisermarsch. 3. Lohengrin. 4. Meistersinger. Close, Tristan. Hope clear. WAGNER.

In the night between the 16th and 17th December, Wagner arrived at Mannheim from Bayreuth. The members of the Wagnerverein had assembled in the station, and welcomed him with a thundering "Hoch!"

"Nay, I'm no prince!" he merrily shouted to us. Then he asked for me, and when we had reached the hotel "zum Europäischen Hof" he seized me by both shoulders, with the words : "Let me see at last what the man of energy looks like."

The ensuing days were full of exciting incidents.

The bandsmen of the Mannheim and Carlsruhe orchestras had agreed to give their services for nothing. When I informed Wagner that Vincenz Lachner would present the united orchestra to him at the first rehearsal, he jumped up from his chair and cried : "Heckel, you ought not to have put *that* upon me. I shall leave at once!—Men like these Lachners wreak their worst on me and my works, for years. I come to their vicinity, and they're the first to thrust themselves upon me." It took me a long time to pacify the justly irate man. The *committee* of the Mannheim theatre had made it a condition of their sanction to the orchestra, that Lachner should retain the privilege of introduction.

Wagner conducted from memory. At the first rehearsal he suddenly broke off, during the Prelude to *Tristan und Isolde*, with the words :

"What's this ? I know no farther."

For the next rehearsal we had the score despatched from Carlsruhe. But he merely looked up that one passage, without needing the score any longer.

Frau Wagner, escorted by Nietzsche, had arrived at Mannheim a few hours after the master.

The main rehearsal itself was attended by visitors not only from the surrounding country, but also from considerable distances. The concert, at which the Grand Duke Friedrich of Baden and the Grandducal family were also present, aroused the liveliest enthusiasm, tumultuously expressed from the very beginning, after the *Kaisermarsch*. This March was originally intended by Wagner for the triumphal Entry of the Troops into Berlin. The Folk's-chant was to be sung by the troops themselves before the Kaiser. Military regulations, however, did not permit the realising of this scheme, and Wagner found himself obliged to adapt the March for the concert-room. Here he laid great stress on *a portrayal of the entry*, so that the piece transformed itself under his baton into a dramatic scene, as it were.

In his article, " A Wagner-concert at Mannheim," [1] Richard Pohl has given a full report of the concert and the banquet that followed it, when Wagner replied at length to an address by the chairman of the Verein, Dr. Zeroni. Enthusiastic cheers succeeded Wagner's words : " The Mannheimers were the first to confirm my belief in the practicability of my plan ; they have shewn me where to seek the true footing for the German artist : in the heart of the nation. Its very name denotes *Mannheim* as the ' *Home of Men*.' Bayreuth, on the other hand, is

[1] Pohl : Richard Wagner, Studien und Kritiken (Bernh. Schlicke, Leipzig).

as yet inviolate, a truly virgin soil for Art.   From
the union of the two should spring a new art-life,
with all the strength of youth.   This is my confident
hope, and I therefore drink to the health of my
friends in Mannheim, the first founders and officers
of the 'Wagner-Verein!'"

During those days the zeal of the executants
would often wax red-hot, in spite of their diametric-
ally opposite training by Lachner.   Concertmeister
N. K. of the Mannheim theatre, a Dutchman by
birth, alone maintained a hostile attitude.   Nevertheless he refused to yield the conduct of the sing-
ing-clubs who had combined to serenade the master,
but entered the room at their head ; which made
Wagner ask, with comical surprise : "Are they going
to guy me, then?"

On the other hand, it transpired how little one
might expect of those "Wagnerians" who merely
went the way of the wind.   At the banquet several
Mannheim citizens of good standing actually declined to take their place at Wagner's table ; they
didn't wish to be viewed as belonging to the stricter
communion.   So the halt, the lame and the blind
sat snugly on one side, without their hearts partici-
pating in our enthusiasm.   Our devotion to the
genius may have driven us to many a reckless step,
both then and thereafter ; but the general resistance
demanded it.   Not alone the bringing-in of fresh
adherents, but even the impotent growls of the
adversary, we took as signs of victory in this battle.

This was no secret to Wagner ; and in this sense,

speaking of the helpers in his undertaking, he grasped my hand at the banquet with the characteristic remark " — *and here the Heckel who annoys some people.*"—

The "private composition" mentioned in Wagner's letter of the 6th December 1871, and not made public until seven years later, as the " Siegfried Idyll," was twice performed at Mannheim under the master's baton on December 20, 1871. Besides Frau Wagner, Nietzsche, Alexander Ritter and wife, Pohl and Nohl, there were present the executive of the Wagnerverein together with Friedr. Wengler and Kapellmeister Handloser.

Between this performance and its publication, I believe the Idyll was played but once, namely in 1877 at the Court of Meiningen.

*　　*

*

Through a letter of Pohl's I knew that Baden-Baden, too, had tried to get the Festival-house erected there, but Wagner was determined to hold fast to Bayreuth. On a map of the town, which he had brought with him, he shewed us the site proposed for the theatre, and told us that the activity of the Mannheim Verein and its public announcement of the concert as for the benefit of a *National theatre at Bayreuth*, had done much to reassure the trust of people there in the undertaking.

Upon his arrival at Mannheim, Wagner had already informed me that he had written something special for me, to wit a "Report to the German Wagner-Verein." This essay has been embodied in the *Gesammelte Schriften* (vol. vi. 367 *et seq.* and vol. ix. 371 *et seq.*), with exception of the closing paragraph.[1]

On the evening of December 21, Wagner started for home.

The success of the Mannheim concert had set the enemy on the alert, and led to the circulation of various rumours, one of which was most emphatic, viz. that Wagner had fallen dangerously ill of typhus at Bâle on his journey back. Upon inquiring of Professor Nietzsche, I received the following telegram:—

Rumour absolutely unfounded; best news from Tribschen. Heartiest New Year's wishes to Wagner-verein. PROFESSOR NIETZSCHE.

In his next few letters, Wagner sends repeated greetings to the "five righteous." In the concert-days he had employed the term to denote the executive of the Mannheim Wagnerverein. Beyond this collective term, he had bestowed a distinctive name on each of us. Dr. Zeroni, whose eloquence in the address after the concert had much delighted him, was called "the Speaker"; Ferdinand Langer, who had been affected in his position at the Mann-

---

[1] Heckel here prints the paragraph whereof an English rendering will be found in a footnote to page 260 of the third volume of *Richard Wagner's Prose Works.*—TR.

heim Court-theatre by his Wagnerism, he christened
" the Reprimanded " ; Hänlein, whom he had already
seen at Tribschen, " the Tribschener " ; Koch " the
Master of Ceremonies," and myself " the Strategos."
Just as in every serious discussion, so in the uncon-
straint of private life, his purely artistic mode of view
rebelled against the dogmatism of abstract terms.
With the most delicious humour and keenest sense
of the situation he would scare away all pedantry,
and make straight for people's hearts.—

For the new year, as " the year of the foundation-
stone of the National theatre at Bayreuth," we telegraphed the good wishes of the Wagnerverein,
having already conveyed our heartiest thanks for the
concert by letter. To my request that he would
name a suitable person to give lectures on his works
and aims, Wagner replied in his next letter :—

To the Five Righteous, greeting and blessing !
Have thanks, dear friends, for your loyal zeal !
Everything was splendid,—only, my old friend R. Pohl
should have known to express himself better. " Self-
intelligible " [1] proves that he hasn't read " German Art and
German Policy " attentively enough.—There our Herr
" Speaker " had the best of him.—By now you will have
received my " Report etc." But you will be more expressly
concerned with what I am saying in a " Communication to
the W.-Vereins "—in the 2nd number of the Musik. Wochenblatt. I fancy it will be of help to you—and consequently
to us.
Glad am I to hear of the " massive " state of things.

---

[1] In his review of the concert, Pohl had used the word " selbstverständlich,"
condemned by Wagner in the work above-named.

I'm building on it, there at Bayreuth, and don't know if we shan't be left in a hole at the last. Everybody must be prepared to commit the common purse in May to my excellent banker Feustel at Bayreuth. For that matter, I see that I shall have to begin to put in a word myself, to give the thing a centre. I imagine the "Righteous" will agree with me.—Naturally the admirable Loën could only be conductor for the first stage.

Lectures ?—My God !—Very good ! But who's to lecture ? In any case he would need a finer voice than X of W.,—he might also be less tedious. That's a terrible person (between our six selves) !

The soul and intellect for such a thing might be found in H. Porges of Munich. Possibly he might be persuaded. You'd better write and tell him that I've recommended him. I fancy he's somewhere in Augsburg just now. Franz Mrazeck, 3 Wittelsbacher Platz (my Munich address) would know where a letter would find him.—

For the rest, I'm living on the handsome expectations of the German National spirit to which I am referred on every hand.—

What gives me joy, is people like yourselves, honoured friends : you know what—and why. The rest may go hang, like the pious speech of Herr Km. Lachner !

A thousand thanks for all the friendly tokens of your kindness and affection ; I have received them with much emotion !

Once more, the heartiest greetings of
Yours faithfully
RICHARD WAGNER.

(formerly ward of the " European Court.")

LUCERNE, 3rd January, 1872.

P.S.—If I do not greet the Righteous in the explicit name of my wife, it is on the supposition that they know—

by experience—I do nothing whatever without her,—so that she is everywhere in all I utter.

R. W.

The above allusion to " Lachner's pious speech " refers to a personal remark of Lachner's that, in presenting the orchestra, he had lost the thread of his discourse and forgotten several " small points."

It was with great delight that we found in his " Communication to the German Wagnervereins " that Wagner had most cordially mentioned " the pre-eminently active friends of his art at Mannheim." [1] His warning against the Vereins being ever " confused with an association for carrying on a speculative business " was chiefly prompted by Nietzsche, who feared lest the ideality of the great undertaking, so strictly maintained by the master himself, might be obscured in the eyes of the public by any semblance of a monetary propaganda. [2]

I wrote begging Wagner to present me with the manuscript of either this " Communication " or the " Report to the German Wagnerverein." I was able at the same time to give him news of fresh connections in various towns.

Frau Wagner answered my petition :—

" Dear Herr Heckel, I will send you one of the manuscripts, albeit with a heavy heart, for I am collecting every morsel of my husband's papers for our son.

---

[1] The " Mittheilung an die deutschen Wagner-Vereine " appeared in the *Musikalisches Wochenblatt* for Jan. 5, 1872 ; it has not been embodied in Wagner's *Gesammelte Schriften.*—Tr.

[2] See Karl Heckel, " Richard Wagner und Friedrich Nietzsche : eine Betrachtung aus der Vogelschau " (Neue Deutsche Rundschau 1896, viii.).

— — — If I say that it is with a heavy heart I send it, you must not misunderstand me ; I know no one to whom I would so gladly make it away, as yourself, who have rendered such good service to the cause."—

A few days later, Frau Wagner sent me the manuscript "Eine Mittheilung an die deutschen Wagner-Vereine." It comprises six closely-written quarto pages, and various alterations prove it to be the first draft.

On January 22, 1872, I received the following telegram from Lucerne :—

Could you forthwith undertake a longish journey of great importance, as my attorney ? If so, first come to me for precise instructions and authority.

Wagner.

My answer ran :—

"Whither ? And how long will journey take? Beg for indications of object, to judge thereby the time and whether I am suited for the honourable mission.—Emil Heckel."

On January 24 I telegraphed again :—

"After receipt of your telegram everything arranged. Awaiting answer : quite ready, soon as know duration of journey.—Emil Heckel."

Frau Wagner replied to this :—

"Wagner already started. Letter coming ; friendly greetings."

Then came Wagner's letter also :—

Esteemed Friend,

I saw that you were not prepared, and am starting to-day myself—to Berlin (if particulars are necessary—for *a conference with my architect*).

Meanwhile, however, please note my pressing request to call in the Patronat-moneys amassed by you, and send the proceeds to Cohn at Dessau.—Further news ere long.

Berlin address :

    Kammergerichtsreferendar Karl von Gersdorff,
        Alexanderstr. 121, 1 Tr. rechts.
          With hearty greetings,
            Your

                R. WAGNER.

LUCERNE, 24*th January*, 1892.

I wrote the master that the words " a longish journey " had led me to assume that a lengthy absence from Mannheim would be requisite, and that would have necessitated certain provisory arrangements in my business. At like time I declared my readiness to prove my zeal by act whenever the occasion offered. Wagner's next letter contained an answer to the question whether the subscription-funds already put out at interest should be withdrawn at once.

Honoured Friend,

The cash itself will probably not be needed for the moment ; but I beg you to send *by return of post* to banker Friedrich Feustel at Bayreuth an exact specification of the state of your Verein (you lately wrote of 16 Patronat-vouchers), so that it may be entered in the register. By the time your letter arrives I myself shall be at Bayreuth, where I am setting up an energetic Central-management of my affair, as it was high time to quit the dilettantism of hitherto.

Hearty thanks for your willingness to undertake the journey. If you preserve this spirit, you may render us *great* services. Before all, I beseech you to obtain me as accurate a list as possible of the existing Wagnervereins, with their addresses. Should conferences be necessary, I shall count on you. More another time. Hearty greetings to the Righteous!

Yours faithfully,
RICHARD WAGNER.

BERLIN, 28*th Jan.* 1872.

As the time approached for commencing the festival-house, Wagner had inquired of both Baron von Loën at Weimar, and Court-banker Cohn at Dessau, the available amount of funds. The number of Patronat-vouchers communicated by both gentlemen exceeded expectations. On his visit to Berlin, however, Wagner found to his great disappointment that each of these two representatives had included the figures of the other, so that the sum disposable was reduced to the half.

I expressed my readiness to come to Bayreuth for a conference, and fulfilled that promise on receipt of Wagner's telegraphic answer:

> *Your coming hither most welcome. Expecting you.*
>
> *Richard Wagner.*

The master then established the "Central Management" at Bayreuth already mentioned in his letter from Berlin, and thus created the long-desired point of union for the Patrons and Vereins. In Burgomaster Muncker, Banker Feustel and Royal-advocate Kaefferlein of Bayreuth, he found good friends to undergo the labour of the central business-control, and friends whose excellence has well been proved.

The preliminaries for the building were now settled. The site on the Stuckberg which the town proposed to give the master for erection of the play-house, but afterwards exchanged for that on the Hohe Warte, had his entire approval. When I returned to Wagner from an inspection of the site, and praised its beauty, he found my words too luke-warm. "Transporting, bewitching, is the name for it," he shouted out. "How sober a Mannheimer can be in his verdict!"

From Bayreuth I went on to Leipzig, for an interview with the committee of the local Wagner-verein, and thence to Berlin. Here I visited Herr L. . . , who shewed me a number of non-obligatory signatures in his notebook, amounting in all to 60,000 thalers, but gave me to understand that they would not be made effective without the fulfilment of certain conditions, such as the transference of the Festspiels to Berlin and so on. Herr L. . ., who dis-played much eagerness to help the cause in his own fashion, had already laid his proposals before Baroness Schleinitz. He offered to start a lottery, and begged me, despite my unconcealed antipathy to that sort of means, to write Wagner to that effect.

I informed Wagner of Herr L. . . 's plan by letter, and, as was only to be expected, received an answer emphatically repudiating the proposal :—

Dear Righteous,
        Thanks once more for your visit to Bayreuth, also for the recent news of your Berlin adventure ! To come at once to the most serious point in the latter regard, I beg you —as Herr L. expects to learn my opinion through yourself —to acquaint this patron that in no case will I give my consent to his projected lottery.

There really can be nothing more disheartening than the position into which I have been lured by exaggerated reports of the standing of a " Wagneriana " in Berlin, as they made me rely on help from a quarter which has proved to be a quicksand.

If anybody will offer me 200,000 th. for the realisation of my ideas, I shall be very grateful to the individual who pays it down ; but to ask my authorisation for a lottery, after the experiences I have had of the " Wagneriana," to me appears a downright swindle, from which I should reap nothing save the scandal, while Herr L. would be left with the reputation for an acquaintance with a distinguished lady to which I should like to see a speedy end put.—

—Premature at least, good friend, I also think (tho' for different reasons than the Leipziger's) the invocation of a Verein whose tendence should aim beyond the immediate and so hardly-attainable goal of a first performance of my Bühnenfestspiel.

The care for this immediate goal will tax all our present forces : I shall reach it, if people stand by me patiently ; my only trouble here concerns my dependence on the King of Bavaria.—

I am already canvassing for the 9th Symphony, and expect definite news ere long about the bandsmen. If the

To Emil Heckel 33

foundation-laying goes off well, according to my programme,
I hope for much assistance from the impression made
thereby.—

Best greetings to the five colleagues in righteousness !
A happy reunion in Bayreuth !

Your heartily faithful

RICHARD WAGNER.

LUCERNE, 16th Feb. 1872.

On Wagner's behalf Herr Concertmeister Will of
Carlsruhe begged me to obtain the co-operation of
several Mannheim bandsmen for the performance of
the Ninth Symphony. In fulfilment of this wish I
secured leave for them through Herr Aug. Scipio,
member of the Court-theatre Committee.

Dear Friend,

Brief and to the point !

Six of your musicians, will be too few for me : I
would gladly have *four* more, among them a good viola-
player.

How are your horns ?

Best thanks for the intervention of Scipio Africanus !—

The Carlsruher are still behindhand.—The promptest
have been Berlin and Vienna ; they are sending me their
élite !—

To cheer your heart :—

Herr W. H. Riehl[1] will soon get a placard from me, to
wear for his Mannheim lectures. You'll be glad.

Greet the Righteous from the bottom of my heart.
Long live Zeroni, were it only for sake of his beautiful

---

[1] Riehl had recommended the founding of "Opposition-clubs" in Mannheim,
against Wagner and his friends. [The "placard" was a reproduction in the
Musik. Wochenblatt for March 22 of an article which had originally appeared in
the *Süddeutsche Presse* of 1867—see *Prose Works*, vol. iv. 253.—TR.]

D

name !   Ah, if *we* were only called so : what do *you* say ?
But — " Wagner," " Heckel " —insupportable !— God will
bless us all, however, you'll see !—

Your

RICHARD WAGNER.

LUCERNE, 15*th March*, 1872.

On the occasion of the master's removal from
Lucerne to Bayreuth the " founders of the first
Wagnerverein " sent the master a complimentary
telegram.

Most valued Friend,
        My heartiest thanks to the " righteous " for their
lovely greeting, which I could not reply to at once in all the
turmoil of removal and preparation for the festival.
    In the pressure of business merely this, to confirm our
arrangements : I count on the following orchestral con-
tingent from Mannheim :

2 first violins	
2 second violins	making 8 musicians, for further com-
1 viola	munications about whom I will
1 violoncello	refer our committee to M[usik]
1 flute (2nd)	d[irekto]r Langer.
1 drummer	

Is that right ?
    Could you lend and send me a *pair of drums* (good
ones) ?—Hardly, I suppose.

Best wishes to the " first beginners,"
To shame of all the " sinners " !—

Wife and child are better here—

On the 5th to Vienna.   Letters to my Council of Management.

Yours,

R. WAGNER.

FANTAISIE, NEAR BAYREUTH, 3rd May 1872.

With Wagner's invitation for the foundation-stone-laying on May 22, 1872, I complied in the highest glee.   I started for Bayreuth as early as the 16th, and stayed as Wagner's guest at the Fantaisie, together with Hans Richter.   The master was in the cheeriest mood, and from the beginning of our drive from the town to the Fantaisie his humour bubbled over.   His favourite dog " Russ," who accompanied him on all his walks, ran merrily beside the carriage. Wagner prized the faithful attachment of this hound unspeakably highly.   When it died he buried it in his garden, next to the vault intended for himself, giving it a gravestone with the words : " Here rests and watches Wagner's Russ."   Wagner's love for his domestic animals was truly touching.

In the evening at the Fantaisie the master sang and played to us, at the pianoforte, the just completed " Hagen's summons to the clansmen."   His voice was mostly full and strong, and attained the proposed dramatic effect with drastic energy and distinctness.

At the rehearsals of the Ninth Symphony in the old Margraves' Operahouse we had fresh examples of his matchless power of working up the executants to feats above their usual level.   At the beginning of the quartet, when Niemann called down to him from the so-called "trumpeters' box" where the soloists were stationed : "Master, if you don't beat time for me here, I cannot sing," Wagner answered, " I shall not beat time—for it would make the rendering stiff. You must sing this passage with absolute freedom. Such an eminent artist as yourself must be able to. That's why I chose you and the others for the quartet. I paint it for you in the air." At the unison for the 'celli and double-basses he said : "Gentlemen, you must know this by heart now. Look at me. There is no beating time. I draw it for you in the air. It must speak like a recitative." The effect was marvellous.

To Professor Riedel's question : "Do we sing 'Was die Mode *frei* getheilt' ? " he answered : "We sing '*frech* getheilt,' "[1] and in his intonation there was an echo, as it were, of the ire with which Beethoven himself may have effected that amendment.

Wherever feasible, Frau Wagner relieved the master of all unpleasant tasks. A Berlin journalist had telegraphed to his paper a false report about Bismarck and the Bayreuth undertaking. It was scarcely to be expected that a simple démenti would obviate the possibility of harmful consequences. When the reporter presented himself at the house of Banker Feustel, where we had assembled before setting out to lay the stone, Frau Wagner asked

[1] " What the Mode did freely part," " What the Mode had *dared* to part "; the original, however, is " streng "—" with rigour,"—not " frei."—Tʀ.

Nietzsche and myself to step into the anteroom, to be witnesses of a dismissal. Here, with the utmost dignity and tact, she gave the culprit a lecture on the disgracefulness of a piece of conduct which spread false rumours for sensation's sake without regard to the fate of a great enterprise. The man quite lost his countenance, complied with every stipulation, and left Bayreuth. Frau Wagner had expressed with moving eloquence my inmost thoughts and feelings about the relation of a whole people to the genius of his age. It was a solemn prelude to the impressions we were about to receive on the Festspiel hill itself.

At the foundation-laying a splendid picture was presented by Niemann's giant frame, when he suddenly sprang forward, and, the living image of a Wagnerian hero, stretched out the hammer for a mighty blow. The master pressed his hand in deep emotion.

After the ceremony was over, Wagner returned to the town with Nietzsche, von Gersdorff, and myself. He sat in earnest silence, as Nietzsche has so well described it, "with a look plunged deep within." Well might all his life crowd back upon him at this hour, his inner vision see both near and far with equal clearness. But as every mood and thought condensed itself to action, in his works, so now he felt impelled to vent his feelings in a tele-graphic message to " his King," who that morning had sent him a similar greeting with the words : " To-day more than ever I am with you in spirit."

On account of the heavy rain, the meeting adjourned to the old Operahouse. Here Wagner himself took the word. In firm reliance on his German people he spoke the "Festival address" (*Ges. Schr.* ix. 388)[1] so clearly, calmly and persuasively, that his undaunted confidence found its way into the heart of every hearer. The designation which I had used in connection with the Mannheim concert, "National theatre at Bayreuth," he disallowed in this speech, for "Where is the Nation, to erect itself this theatre?" Yet he described the building as hallowed by "the German Spirit that shouts to us across the centuries its ever young Good-morrow."

Nietzsche has reproduced the impressions of these days in his "Unzeitgemässe Betrachtung : Richard Wagner in Bayreuth." Later too, when antagonism of aims had severed their paths, he spoke with warmth of "the incomparable days of the foundation-laying and the little, homogeneous company that celebrated it."

*   *

*

— — After my return to Mannheim I conveyed to Wagner the offer of two enthusiastic bandsmen and a painter relative of mine, to assist in the festivals. As regards the latter, whose mounting of the *Flying Dutchman* at Mannheim was fully approved by Wagner later, the master sent me a letter of Karl Brandt's, adding to it the following words :—

[1] *Richard Wagner's Prose Works*, v. 324-8.—Tr.

To Emil Heckel 39

Dearest Friend,

You see—what Brandt writes me ! Don't be cross with me, but—you will see that I took note of your request, and made inquiries of my adviser !—As to the bandsmen, it surely is a wee bit early. Children, children ! I've other lambs to tend first !—

For the present the Call has been, just what you write about it !—

In a little while the Mannheimers also shall get a reminder of Bayreuth and   my
                                            Insignificance,
which most heartily commends itself to you and the five Righteous.

FANTAISIE, 15th June 1872, evening.

*   *

Best Friend,

One can never be too careful ! Again it has happened to me, that—down to the receipt of Brandt's letter—I had forgotten that your nominee was your brother-in-law, and—quite unintentionally—I have had the indelicacy to send you disagreeable news about a near relation !—

But indeed, friend—in my present state of turmoil and preoccupation—too many questions, and the like, are put to me ; so I get confused and out of sorts, and dash things off just as they come.

For that matter—there's plenty of time for the scenery ! I need a few months more for my work ; then I shall be looking around in Germania, to right and left, and shall certainly come to you in Mannheim too, when God will fix the rest.—

If you preserve me your friendship, that must suffice for the present to

Yours sincerely
RICHARD WAGNER.

BAYREUTH, 22nd June '72.

In accordance with an earlier promise, Frau Wagner sent me photographs of the master for the "five righteous." In my letter of thanks I invited Wagner to put up at my house, should he be coming to Mannheim. At like time I informed Frau Wagner that I was anxious to enrol the "truest Wagnerians" with the 448 members of the Mannheim Wagnerverein, the "Mother-union" as Hans Richter had styled it. Frau von Schleinitz having acceded to a similar wish, I begged Frau Wagner to join our Verein. Her kind acceptance soon arrived; also that of Franz Liszt, to whom I had addressed the same petition :—

Dear Herr Heckel,
        With all my heart I join the Verein; you must remind me of my duties, that is to say, the time when I have to fulfil them.
        Wagner would accept your very kind offer with great delight—but, dear Herr Heckel, would you be able to take me in as well? Not that I want anything at all out of the way, but I do not know how you are off for room in your dwelling, and whether your good wife will care to receive two guests for one.
        The building of the theatre goes briskly on, and the Magistrates' recent—and most solemn—permission to sell sausage on the premises, has afforded us much delectation.
        Hearty greetings from house to house !
                                        COSIMA WAGNER.

FANTAISIE, 11*th* *July* 1872.

Honoured Sir,
        Incessant interruptions have delayed my thanks for your obliging letter re the Mannheim *Wagner-Verein* until to-day.

When Tausig first informed me, in May last year, of the great project for performing the Nibelungen at Bayreuth, I signed at once three Patronat-vouchers. Unfortunately, my scanty income does not permit my making a more considerable contribution. However, as I have been associated with the Leipzig Wagnerverein since last year, as member of the "Allgemeiner deutsche Musikverein," and as you so kindly invite me to join your Mannheim "Mutterverein," I beg leave to forward the subscription of 15 gulden (for the years 1871, 72 and 73—according to the statutes).

Receive, most honoured Sir, the assurance of my particular estimation of your energetic services on behalf of the Wagner-Vereins, and the expression of my sincere devotion.

F. Liszt.

Weimar, 17. *September '72.*

I besought Liszt to resume his concert-giving, for the benefit of Bayreuth and the joy of all musicians, in the conviction that the undertaking would thus reap great assistance. Unfortunately this wish was not fulfilled.

At that time I was in active correspondence with Hans von Bülow also, who stood prepared to come to Mannheim and take up Lachner's post. But at the last moment Lachner decided to withdraw his application for a pension, and thus frustrated the proposed reform of the Mannheim Court-theatre.[1]

* *

*

[1] See Karl Heckel " Hans von Bülow's Plan eines deutschen Nationaltheaters " (Neue Deutsche Rundschau vii. 11).

On the 10th November 1872 Wagner and his wife commenced a long tour of Germany, to inspect the various operatic companies. Beyond the succeeding letters I received several telegrams in which he acquainted me, first with a delay in his departure for Wurzburg, then with the hour of his arrival at Mannheim.

Best Friend,
    If—without too much trouble to yourself—you could acquaint me with the Mannheim operatic repertoire —perhaps also the Carlsruhe—from about next Sunday, your news would meet me at Wurzburg (Conzertmeister A. Ritter), whither I am bound on Wednesday, and where I expect like news from Darmstadt. Whichever theatre may then come first—according to the attraction it offers me—in any case you will see me soon, and I hope the dear Righteous have not become meanwhiles unrighteous.
                        With heartiest greeting,
                            Yours faithfully
                                RICHARD WAGNER.
    BAYREUTH, *Monday, 4. Nov.* 1872.

Dear Friend,
    After counting all the chances offered me, for whose multiplication I heartily thank you, we think of taking acoustic stock of the "Flying Dutchman" at your place next Sunday. For this we shall arrive on *Friday* from Frankfort, and stop till Monday morning, so that you may dispose of me for that length of time in all-righteous fashion.
    In thankful old friendship,
                        Your faithful
                            RICHARD WAGNER.

    WURZBURG, 11. *Nov.* '72.

Your tidings please send me at Frankfort, poste- or station-restante.

On the 15th November Wagner and his wife arrived at Mannheim. Alighted in my house, he first insisted upon seeing all the rooms, to convince himself that my family had not been too much cramped for his sake.

Prompted by my brother C. F. Heckel, its president, the "Liedertafel" serenaded Wagner next morning.

In the evening we attended Nohl's lecture on "The German Musicdrama." This title of Nohl's gave Wagner occasion to protest against both it and the appellation "Musical Drama," in his well-known article. For my part I consider Chamberlain's choice of "German Drama," in the sense assigned it by that author, the most appropriate. *One alone could create it!* however many may think they could to-day.

After the lecture, Wagner spent the rest of the evening in my family-circle.

On the following day he again was greeted with a musical good-morning. The horn-quartet of the Court-theatre played the Preislied and the "Wach' auf" chorus from the *Meistersinger*, arrangements by Ferd. Langer, copies of which Frau Wagner afterwards got me repeatedly to send her. Wagner was delighted with a hearty and intelligent little speech by the flautist Neuhofer, a staunch adherent of his cause.

In my music-room Wagner played us the recently-composed "Norns' scene" and "Siegfried's Rhein-fahrt." Seeing my eyes fixed on his fingers, he said in joke: "Oh, you must watch me closely. Look! I don't do as other pianists, who put their thumbs below; no, you see I cross them *over* my fingers." At our "morning glass," too, which we took at 12 o'clock each day, he was always brimming over with fun.

Before his visit to the theatre we had informed him of Lachner's cuts in the *Flying Dutchman;* but they so far passed his expectation that he left the theatre in a fury after the second act, taking no notice of the audience's clamour for a sight of him. The very fact of Lachner's playing the overture without its later-added close had irritated, but the arbitrary omissions in the second act especially en-raged him, as in these he saw intentional disfigurement.

He paid great attention to the auditorium, which had been transformed by my father-in-law, Joseph Mühldorfer, so that a space, quite empty at the sides, was left between the audience and the stage, with a view to isolating the scenic picture. Thereafter Wagner expressed himself at length about this "excellent idea of the builder's" (*Ges. Schr.* ix. 402 [1]). In earlier years he had entered into direct communication with Mühldorfer (who died in 1863), as he relates in a letter to a Viennese friend:—

"I decided to send the book [of the *Ring*] to the famous

---

[1] *Prose Works*, v. 335, footnote.—Tr.

scene-painter Gropius of Berlin and the talented stage-machinist Mühldorfer of Mannheim (inventor of the moving scenery for 'Oberon'), asking them if its stage-directions were technically executable. Both of them, ambitious representatives of their profession, replied 'O yes, it can all be done.'"

* *

*

Wagner had the quick eye of a satirist for the absurdity of self-conceit. As he was sitting at the window of my house, correcting the proofs of the *Meistersinger* poem [for *Ges. Schr.* vol. vii.], it highly amused him to see a tall gaunt figure gravely stalking to and fro in the opposite house, and trying to attract his attention by a book of poetry in a brilliant crimson cover. It was Court-theatre-president R., who had declined to take notice of Wagner till the latter should have paid him a visit "as in duty bound." Little as Wagner asked for any kind of servility from the naïve man, as sharply did he lash the pretentious humbug of people of no real distinction in exalted stations. The German philistines and their mouthpiece, on the contrary, have always turned their taunts against the genius and his works; for "to mock at the sublime, at anyrate seems easier than to shew the fatuous in all its solemn ridicule" [*Prose Works*, iv. 254].

The Lachner-cuts were a frequent topic of conversation, often of an humorous nature. Thus it happened that Musikdirektor Langer had to leave us one evening, to conduct the then still customary

" entr'acte music " at the theatre.   Wagner asked
him what he was going to play, and upon Langer's
answering that there were a few suitable arrangements, but nothing like enough, the master cried :
" Do you know what ?   If you'd only play everything that people cut out of my works, it would last
you for years."

Of high interest were Wagner's tales about his
life and interviews with noted men.   Thus he related
me a long story of his visit to Bismarck, and how
the latter had told him that everybody knew his
work below, in the unifying of Germany, but few
people knew what labour had been needed above,
here and there, before the head-piece (*Pickelhaube*)
had come by a hole to let in the German idea.   At
dinner he drank Bismarck's health with me.

One evening we supped at Zeroni's.   Wagner
replied to the toast of his health in such a fervent
tone, and spoke so movingly, that our eyes were
moistened.   Later he sang us portions of the
Meistersinger, at first alone, then with Langer (whose
delivery he very much liked) the " dialogue between
Hans Sachs and Evchen."   When Hänlein and
Zeroni played the *Kaisermarsch* he joined lustily in
the closing chorus.

The next morning, after we had discussed various
questions concerning the Bayreuth undertaking, he
gave me his new pamphlet " On Actors and Singers,"
and wrote on its cover a dedication which I prize as
a token of hearty acknowledgment.   It runs :—

To Emil Heckel

If each pot had its Deckel, [lid]
Every Wagner his Heckel,
Man might live without trouble,
And the world be no bubble !
                    RICHARD WAGNER,
                Visitor cut in Mannheim,
                    19. *Nov.* 1872.

The allusion to the cuts in the *Flying Dutchman*, after the signature, is repeated with the humorous verses which he wrote on the back of a photograph of his wife :—

Frau Cosima in the best humour,
And no one shall call it a rumour :
For she has a good man,
And compose well he can.
So her faithful memento
To the Heckels she's sent O !
                        Mannheim poem,
            by the author of the Flying Dutchman
                    without cuts.

On another photograph, intended for the family-circle alone, and shewing the master and his wife looking into one another's eyes, he wrote : " Long life to all the Heckelei !   Richard and Cosima, here the good couple are ! "

Wagner offered to conduct *Lohengrin* and the *Magic Flute* at Mannheim, if I could only get things done according to his wish.   He also declared himself ready to dispute in public about his art, if a fit opponent could be found.   Neither plan came to anything.

As a rule we rose of a morning before our good

guests.   Once, however, Wagner went to the pianino quite early, and played the Pilgrims'-chorus from *Tannhäuser*.   It delighted him to have roused us from our morning slumbers.   O yes! the earnest man could be as lively as anyone.—Difficult as it is, to reproduce in writing the many characteristic touches of natural gaiety in Wagner's daily intercourse, I should like to lay especial stress on them ; for in none of the many biographies have I found his genial humour, and his artistry in private life, sufficiently appreciated.

On November 20 the Wagners left us, to pursue their journey ; but I met them a few days later at the Mannheim station again, as the master had telegraphed me that he would be passing through, and wished to relate a conversation he had had with the Grand Duke of Baden.

His next news came from Wiesbaden and Cologne :—

WIESBADEN, *the* 28*th November* 1872.

Dear Friend and Comrade,

I am taking a moment's rest, to see whether I owe anybody a letter, and so I find it well to remind you most urgently to place yourself in as agreeable communication as possible with Feustel of Bayreuth.   We discussed that before.   Tell him exactly what you hold at his disposal now, and how much more will be available for him at Easter.   If payments are made to yourself, as recently through Fräulein Nietzsche, please send them on at once to Feustel.   I know from his latest report that he regards the progress of our undertaking with anxiety if he doesn't get reassuring news and, above all, advances.

To-night I am to meet the Mayence W.-V.   At
Cologne a similar meeting is under way. (At Mainz this
evening: Zauberflöte.)   In all probability I shall not go to
Cologne before Saturday.   There (Lesimple) I should be
glad of any news.   Hearty greetings to yourself, the wife,
the friends of my wife and her husband.

RICHARD WAGNER.

*   *

COLOGNE, 1. *December '72.*

My dear friend Heckel,
my work-pot's Deckel!

Herewith I send the papers back,
And hope we all may have no lack!

On the Main
O 'twas fine
in the Wagnerverein!—
Music-corps 'hind and before'n,
all blowing the Bayreuther horn!
In Cologne it is equally great,
where splendid affairs we await:
the Wagnervereinian choir
to a lecture by me doth aspire.
Till Thursday I mean to stop here,
then go on to the easterly sphere.
All your sins of omission
shall obtain their remission,
If you fill the pence-bowl;
for the good of your soul!

R. W.
as Monk Detzel.

During the next few months our business was

E

transacted through the indefatigable Feustel, whilst personal and domestic questions were discussed by letter with Frau Wagner.

Upon my informing Wagner that Lachner's successor at Mannheim, Ernst Frank, at my request had given *Lohengrin* unmutilated, he wrote on March 17, 1873, from Bayreuth :—

> Look out !   Here comes a lovely poem !
> Attention—:—
>
> Long live the Kapellmeister Frank !
> Now let him purge the music-bank,
> which of the cutter's person stank,
> and sit there so that we may thank !
> E'en Wagner's scores and parts so crank
> shall stand before him free and frank :
> however oft, when them he drank,
> they made poor Vincenz lean and lank,—
> Patroclus to the grave once sank :
> my cry is : Long live P. P. Frank !
>   R. W.
>   (poeta !)

Frank, in effect, then rid us of numerous cuts in the *Meistersinger*, and won his laurels by producing for the first time Götz's opera *The Taming of the Shrew*, to which Bülow had drawn my attention. Later on, however, Ernst Frank found it opportune to let his zeal for Wagner and the new art cool down.

At the "roof-beam feast" at Bayreuth (2nd August 1873) I was not present.   Wagner had issued no personal invitations, as nothing was to take place besides the crowning of the beam itself. A public invitation had gone out to all the Patrons, through advertisement in the newspapers, but had been overlooked by myself, as by most of us.

With a message that he had expected and missed me at the junket, the master at like time asked if I would not visit him in course of the summer, to inspect the progress of the works.

Unfortunately he saw himself compelled to postpone the Festivals, originally announced for 1874. The initial hope that 1000 art-lovers would be found to pay 300 thalers each, to become Patrons of the undertaking, was not fulfilled. The "really rich" in Germany, with few exceptions, met the enterprise with neither artistic generosity nor national interest. The Wagnervereins, on the other hand, addressing themselves chiefly to less wealthy people, only in a few cities were able to collect presentable sums (the Mannheim Verein forwarded 51,000 marks in all), but could never make up for the indifference of those who might have enabled the festivals to become a fact as early as 1874.

In a circular letter Wagner acquainted the Vereins and Patrons with the state of affairs. These confidential communications unexpectedly found their way into the press at once.[1] Wagner's hint that a

[1] The circular is dated Aug. 30, 1873. A short and spiteful article appeared in the Leipzig *Signale für die musikalische Welt* by the middle of September (undated, but the 4th out of 7 numbers for that month); this article is repeated almost textually, but with addition of long quotations from the circular, in the Leipzig *Allgemeine musikalische Zeitung* of Sep. 24, 1873.—Tr.

change in the original tendence might become
necessary, was misconstrued as an intention to turn
the thing into a "limited company." Upon my
informing him that the Mannheim "righteous"
would stand up for unconditional adherence to the
original tendence, he replied :—

Dear Friend Heckel,
        Who once is righteous, remains righteous always!
Have thanks for your amiable tidings. Louis XIV. once
said to Jean Bart :—"I wish I had 500 men like you!"
whereon Jean answered him :—"Sire, I believe you!"
That's about what you might reply to me, were I to wish
for but a dozen Heckels, with his Righteous, in the whole
of Germany.
        For the rest, you all are strangely thick-skinned people!
You think needful to warn me solemnly against turning my
affair into a joint-stock company? That's what seems to
have been the whole drift of my circular? God knows, I
never meant the thing like that; honestly, what I hinted in
that sense, was merely said to shame Germania's public.—
Again I have had the most abominable experience, that,
before I even had a line from anyone to whom the circular
was sent, the whole thing had got into the precious press.
What sort of persons are my Patrons? To run to the
newspaper-hack the very first thing : the lot is only fit for
that!
        Again you have to work against this nuisance—in your
own way ; and you do very well. But in future I shall be
more and more reticent. Write and clap, can the people,—
eh! give advice by the hundred and thousand. But do
anything—do only the Righteous!—
        However, the main thing is to come to a speedy agree-
ment about a better mode of attack : subscriptions must be
started, lists hawked round; few can give 100 thlr. (say,

for a national object), but several 50, still more 20, many 10 thlr., especially such people as can be talked into supporting the thing for its magnitude, without their having special interest enough to undertake the journey to Bayreuth for the performances themselves some day.

You must work out the draft of an organised agitation in this sense, send it me for my approval, as it were, and then make a thorough good blaze of the thing, thus furnished with my sanction ; and with such publicity, that nobody shall be able to say, "But I've heard nothing at all about it ! "—as I so often get for rejoinder just now.

Well, well! I hope to see you here soon. No more concerts will I give. They only do harm : instead of being stirred to further action, people think they've done enough with these concert-takings, and there's an end to the thing. Just so at Cologne, where the Wagner-Verein hasn't brought off the least stroke *in consequence of the concert.* As usual !—

Now greet the Righteous, particularly our wonder-doctor [Zeroni], most heartily from me, as you and your dear wife are greeted by me and mine !

Your
RICHARD WAGNER.

BAYREUTH, 19. *September* 1873.

After receipt of this letter I proposed to Wagner to have subscription-lists exposed in every book and music shop, and offered to despatch them together with an Appeal from the "Mannheimer Wagner-verein." In this Appeal I wished to lay stress on the humiliating fact that *Chicago* and *London* had offered to build Wagner a theatre according to his plans, whilst Germany was still behindhand with its sympathy. His reply deserves particular attention, as it sets his aims and objects clearly forth, and thereby gives an answer to the question : Why Bayreuth ?

Dearest Friend,

The answer to your letter—or rather, proposal—really demanded a little reflection. I have no word to say against whatever method the Mannheim Verein deems best to serve with energy the object for which it was founded: in any case, as it was the first to call the idea of W.-Vereins into life, it is only meet that it should take the initiative, and no one can dispute with it the honour of being the pioneer in this affair. Only, be careful in your boasts about myself: we cannot refer to Chicago and London so unconditionally ; in both cities a new theatre had already been built, and—to be sure—if I had consented to take the thing into my personal hands, it would have been fitted up according to my wishes, also the performers engaged according to my choice. That was for my operas in general. But now we come to the crucial point : in Berlin a "Wagneriana" had been formed, with 220,000 thlr. already underwritten, and the prospect of a million for me, if I would transfer Bayreuth—(with modifications) to Berlin ; the same thing would have been infinitely easier in Vienna, for itself, than to get subscriptions there for Bayreuth. It thus is not demonstrable that people would not have built my theatre in a *large German* capital too, and the crux accordingly resides in my having cast my eye on a neutral spot with an undertaking for the whole German public, not the mere public of one capital. Cities like Chicago, and so on, could perhaps be found in Germany as well, but —— not the *German public.*

As to ventilating a subscription, however, it would perhaps be more advisable that this should be started by a consortium of influential men from the *various* German centres. Here my hands are already tied a little, as a rich

To Emil Heckel 55

and energetic Hamburg merchant (Zacharias, Fontenay 1
—or 2—Hamburg), proposes to convoke such a preliminary
meeting for the 15th October. Would you not place
yourself in correspondence with him? I am sure that he
also would like to address himself to you.

If you proceed to a *manifesto* (which might have a very
good effect), I would really beg you to ask the advice of
Nietzsche at Bâle in its composition ; in any case you might
approach him at once, to draft you such a manifesto. In
this regard I have quite especial confidence in him—in him
of all others.—

Well, we shall see !

A "Max Pauer" of Steyermark (Schloss Gutentag),
wrote me a few days back that he was sending you 200
thlr. to supplement the ⅓ of his patronat-voucher—taken up
through you. Has he done so ?—

I am tired, God knows, but heartily do I greet yourself
and all of yours.

Your faithful
RICHARD WAGNER.

BAYREUTH, 23. *Sept.* 1873.

On receipt of my details about the intended
propaganda, Wagner sent me word to await the
conference which Banker Zacharias of Hamburg
wished to summon. It was to be assumed that a
Patronat-consortium would be formed at this meeting.
If such a body were to decide on signing for substantial sums, it naturally would acquire the right of
addressing a challenge to the German public to
follow its example. The consortium, for which
Wagner had proposed myself as member, was also to
assume a host of other duties.

However, on October 12 I received the following telegram :—

Emil Heckel, Mannheim.

Conference abandoned. Despite feeble interest, meeting of righteous 31 *October, for which circular going out. Greetings.*

Richard Wagner.

Herr Zacharias, who had been the first to suggest the conference, suddenly held himself unqualified to convoke and organise it. The whole grandiloquent offer burst up like a soap-bubble.

Wagner wrote me, on a circular to the Patrons :—

My dear Friend,

The " conference " was another—by word of mouth !

Let us content ourselves now with the meeting of delegates. Even if we are few, we shall at all events represent something—namely, the Wagner-Vereins. In their name a manifesto can very decently go forth. My wife has written you hereon.

Only come, and bring Zeroni with you if possible. My opinion is, things will go right after all.

With the heartiest greetings,

Your faithful

RICHARD WAGNER.

BAYREUTH, 17. *Oct.* 1873.

So I wrote to Nietzsche, at Wagner's instigation, and received his kind consent :—

To Emil Heckel

Most esteemed Herr Heckel,
    What you ask of me, shall be done.
    To me your sketch for the booksellers seems excellent,
as in fact the whole plan proclaims its author.   Let me
keep the sketch * a few days longer, to examine it at leisure ;
by then I perhaps can forward my own with it.   If my
health at all allows, I shall come to Bayreuth on the 30th
inst.   I will get a number of copies of my draft printed
here : that will render it easier to go over, and, if necessary,
revise.

Faithfully yours,
NIETZSCHE.

BÂLE, 19. *October* 1873.

    * No : I return it herewith, and have already looked
through it.

    Nietzsche indited a powerful and outspoken
" Admonition to the Germans," [1] but to our great
astonishment and regret the meeting of delegates did
not deem opportune to issue it, and entrusted Professor Stern of Dresden with the drafting of another
Appeal.   As to further business, the motions to
institute a lottery, etc. were rejected, and my above
proposals passed.
    Wagner then dwelt in the town (Dammallee).
Again I spent many happy hours in his intimate
circle, together with Fräulein von Meysenbug
(authoress of the *Memoirs of an Idealist*), and " Tasso-
Nietzsche."
    I made the return journey *via* Heidelberg in
Nietzsche's company.   After a few days I received
the following telegram :—

[1] Printed in Frau Förster-Nietzsche's *Das Leben Friedrich Nietzsche's*, vol. ii.

*Please send Stern's Appeal soon as possible.   Wel-
come home.   Merry reunion to all the righteous!*

Richard Wagner.

I carried out the resolutions passed at the meeting, and tried in various other ways to serve the
undertaking.   How very grateful Wagner was for
every helping hand, was shewn me again by his next
letter :—

O you most admirable of men !

Accept my warmest thanks for all that you are doing,
into the details of which I have no need to enter now.
You may tell yourself that, if your ways and efforts don't
lead to the goal, nothing else—that is honourable—could
help us to it.

God knows, perhaps you'll even reap some good from
the newspaper-editors : I have remarked that unintelligence
often works more havoc than downright malice !—

To-morrow I shall start for Munich, to see if there still
is hope of the King's intervening.   In the worse event, it
may yet be possible to retain the date of 1875 if this winter
only bears good fruit.   If I can definitely settle with Brandt
and Hoffmann in the spring, they still will have time to get
ready—according to former statements.   At the end of this
month I shall confer with both of them here.

So—we will hope then !   On the path you have struck
with such energy and prudence we yet may find still-hidden
forces of the German nature : this is of almost greater
importance than the success of the undertaking itself.

A thousand hearty wishes to you and yours from myself
and my dear wife !

Your
RICHARD WAGNER.

BAYREUTH, 19. *Nov.* 1873.

To Emil Heckel 59

Nietzsche wrote me about his intention to found a " Swiss Wagner-Verein," and in the following letter Fräulein von Meysenbug informed me of the technical preparations for the Festspiels :—

BAYREUTH, 1. *December* 1873.

You will be surprised, dear Herr Heckel, to receive another letter from me so soon. This time it is at the behest of higher powers. For we have had Herren Brandt and Hoffmann here, and the latter has submitted his sketches for the scenery of the Ring des Nibelungen. These surprised and delighted the master in the highest degree, for they are works of a true artist, who has grasped the poem with profound understanding and will give it the worthy background on which Wagner had reckoned. Where trifling differences of opinion arose, and the author had to ask of the painter the sacrifice of one or other picturesque device, for sake of his poetic intentions, this was fulfilled in the most amiable fashion, and we here had a foretaste of what is some day to be realised with the Artwork of the Future : the co-operation of all the arts to form a perfect whole, without pretentious self-assertion of one or other of them. The best understanding was arrived at, and it was agreed to begin the work in January, at first at Darmstadt, to complete the models with Brandt's assistance, and in March or April to commence the painting of the scenery at Bayreuth, for which purpose Herr Hoffmann will take up residence here.

I give you this brief report as Wagner wishes you to send it (in better language) to a few newspapers, to shew the public that things are really moving forward and the damaging absurdities now circulated in all the papers are false.

Many thanks for transmitting the Appeals, and for your letter.

With best greeting in the sign under which we conquer,
Yours
M. v. MEYSENBUG.

After an intimation that I had sent a circular letter to 81 German theatres, begging them to prove their interest in German art by performances for the benefit of Bayreuth ; also in answer to my petition, to allow me to have excerpts from *Die Walküre* and *Tristan und Isolde* performed at a concert (with the two Vogls), I received a message from Wagner :—

"Once for all, dear Most-righteous, *you* may do or leave undone what you think good, but please don't ask for approbation or consent to the abandonment of a principle (as for instance, the epistle to the Theatre-Intendants, and Walküre fragments).   Grateful shall we be to you for all you undertake, however, since we know well that it comes hard enough to yourself to depart from principles, and you only do it with a view to furthering the cause ; moreover your successes have been great and unexpected enough, to permit you unconditionally to follow your feeling.   Only, as said, do not ask for the master's assent, as he stands or falls with his principles (the concerts, though they brought in much, were yet perhaps of evil) ; his thanks you have for *everything*."

In the period immediately ensuing, the sudden monetary crisis in Austria and Germany had a markedly unfavourable effect on the enterprise ; funds came in slower and slower.   Neither the letters to the Intendants, nor the subscription-lists exposed at the book and music shops, answered expectations.

Certainly there was no lack of advice and enthusiastic
epistles from the most diverse quarters, but only in a
very few towns was a corresponding energy dis-
played.

Wagner hoped the King of Bavaria would undertake a financial guarantee, but Feustel had written me
that unfortunately the King had a pique against
Wagner, the cause of which he could not state by
letter. It therefore boded no good when the
following telegram arrived from Wagner, with which
I complied at once :

*Urgently beg your visit for weighty discussion. Exactest
understanding between us indispensable.*
Dutifully Richard Wagner.

I went immediately to Bayreuth. In place of the
usual active cheerfulness, I now found the deepest
depression. In an "*Open Letter*," which he meant
to address to myself, Wagner proposed to declare
that the undertaking was stranded and we must wait
for better times before proceeding with the building.
He told me : "I'll have the still open walls of the
Festival-house boarded in, that at least the owls
mayn't build their nests there, until we can go on
building again."

I promptly replied: "That shall never be !"
His Bayreuth friends had lost all hope. Not I.
And to-day I am proud of having been able to revive
his trust and confidence, though I could offer nothing
beyond plans and projects opening up new vistas.

It was of the greatest importance that Feustel had told me by mouth, on my arrival, the cause of the King's displeasure. Wagner had emphatically declined a German writer's invitation to set to music a hymn of his called " *Macte Imperator.*" Whether Wagner had not been informed that this request had its origin in a wish of the King's, whether his refusal had been distorted in its reproduction at court, or what other circumstances may have helped a small cause to a great effect, I did not hear. As Feustel had pledged his word of honour to say nothing to Wagner about this matter, I could only give the master one end of the yarn whose unravelling led to fresh hopes.

From Mannheim I wrote to a friend and well-wisher of Wagner's about the starting of a " guarantee-fund," without, however, receiving a serviceable answer. We had further agreed at Bayreuth that, armed with a letter from Wagner, I should endeavour to obtain the Grand Duke of Baden's intervention with Kaiser Wilhelm, that the festivals might be nationally assisted by the Reich as a " *Lustral celebration of the Peace.*" Wagner accordingly wrote the following letter, which I despatched to the Grand-ducal Privy Cabinet at Carlsruhe together with a petition for an audience from myself :—

Dear and Honoured Friend,
    It behoves me to turn to yourself, the most active and effectual founder and fosterer of a society for the furtherance of my intended Bühnenfestspiels, when it concerns a momentous step which can be more fitly taken

by a proved and sagacious friend of my enterprise than by him who has to look upon that enterprise as his own. A powerful aid has become needful to us, if the work begun is to be carried to a speedy termination; whilst everything is bound up in that speedy execution, as it all depends on the retention of my personal bodily strength. In the course of two years we have been provided with as much as one hundred thousand thalers by the more immediate friends of my art: with this money we have laid the durable foundation of the whole undertaking, through erection of a Stage-festival-house whose structural solidity insures its service for any conceivable length of time. Only, at the very latest moment for giving definite orders for the construction of the stage-machinery and decorations, the forces of whilom aiders of the undertaking are quite exhausted; its progress is necessarily suspended, and itself accordingly falls victim to a sorry fate if no authoritative power shall intervene with help.—

My agents here are of opinion that the undertaking should still be pursued at all hazards to the point of actual execution, as we may confidently rely on the costs being covered by the practical outcome of the interest displayed both far and wide in a quite unusual art-event. In this sense we are only in need of a sufficient guarantee, to secure us a loan in provision for uninterrupted continuance of what has been begun. In quest of such a guarantee I lately approached my exalted benefactor, the King of Bavaria; for reasons not clear to myself, His Majesty has decided adversely.

You know that we have lately been seeking such a guarantee among the richest of our willing friends. Yet even should this quarter furnish us assistance, presumably but temporary, for my part I am resolved to seek the rescue of such an important affair in the only place that can confer on it a corresponding dignity.

If I thus am thinking of the " Reich," you are not

unaware how I hitherto have always shrunk from the idea of my undertaking and its fundamental culture-motive being discussed by the deputies to our Reichstag, as I should be unable to find a single one amongst them who could convincingly set forth and represent its proper meaning in face of the shameful disparagement of my project by our altogether ignorant Press of nowadays, both great and small.—No : I have come by the thought of offering to our victorious Kaiser himself the first performances of my work, in lustral celebration of the glorious peace concluded with France in the year 1871.—It therefore would be a question of placing the performance of my Nibelungen-work — effected amid circumstances so novel and peculiar to the German nature—in the same category as those theatric festivals which, pursuant to a not very laudable tradition, have hitherto been made to celebrate such high memorial days : I then should view the acceptance of my offer as alike the recognition of an idea of some moment to German culture.—It would not beseem me to express myself, however, with persuasive force on such a point ; I am absolutely bound to seek among the friends of my art, the well-wishers of my enterprise, for advocates who, guided by my circumstantial brief, can place the importance of my project in the requisite light at head-quarters.

In this, as in every other sense, it is a grand encouragement to me, to be able to select yourself, dear honoured friend, as first spokesman to your country's lord, the Grand Duke of Baden, whom I revere so highly. This pattern German Prince was the first to entertain me and my undertakings with truly luminous good-will in 1861, when I returned to Germany after years of exile. Since then, I have no reason to suspect a cooling of the magnanimous feelings which greeted me at that time, and therefore believe that you will meet a temper profoundly prepared and earnestly disposed in my favour, if you approach His Royal Highness in the name of all who already have lent their forces to my undertaking, among whom I have the special satisfaction of numbering my illustrious benefactor himself, to mediate a decisive aid on the path above outlined.

It cannot be my province to offer more precise suggestions as to the pursuit of this path, if it is resolved upon by the Grand Duke, as it would probably be natural that the co-operation of His Imperial and Royal Highness the Crown Prince of the German Empire might at once be contemplated by my illustrious benefactor as the most efficacious of all. I would merely permit myself to name their Highnesses the Grand Dukes of Saxe-Weimar and Mecklenburg and the Duke of Dessau, who have already evinced their personal interest in my undertaking, as presumably inclined to such co-operation.

To indicate precisely what I figure to myself as the crowning result of so powerful an intervention for my aims and wishes, I aspire to obtaining the Kaiser's command—as against the grant of one-hundred-thousand thalers, that is to say, the third part of the total costs of the undertaking—to institute three complete performances of my Bühnenfestspiel "Der Ring des Nibelungen" at a festival-theatre built at Bayreuth expressly for the purpose, in the summer of 1876 as the first lustral celebration of the peace concluded with France.

As it would be easy to arrive in plain figures at the number of seats to be secured by that sum, on the same scale as the rights of the present Patrons, in this communication to yourself I pass over all details of the business aspect of the matter, and beg you in union with our valued friends at Mannheim to take the first step towards the realisement of my floating idea, which I gladly restore to you as your own property.

With all esteem and friendship,
Yours faithfully,
RICHARD WAGNER.

BAYREUTH, 16. *January* 1874.

F

The Grand Duke of Baden was at all times very partial to Wagner and his art. In particular the Mannheim Wagner-concert had made a great impression on him ; so that the desired aid was surely to be expected from his goodwill. The mischance of certain combinations in party politics, however, occasioned the following refusal :—

Highly-honoured Sir !
    Your much valued communication, enclosing to your humble servant the letter from Herr Richard Wagner dated Bayreuth the 16th January, and requesting that this document be brought to the knowledge of his Royal Highness the Grand Duke with the petition that his Royal Highness would grant you an audience for the purpose of supplementing the contents of the letter addressed to your honour by Herr Richard Wagner, duly reached me. I made no delay in complying with your wish. His Royal Highness has inspected the letter aforesaid, and commands me to inform your honour that he sincerely regrets not being able to accede to the request of Herr Richard Wagner that he should lay the matter of the Bühnenfest-spiel at Bayreuth before His Majesty the German Emperor with the object of obtaining a subsidy from the Reich to ensure the execution of the undertaking. After going thoroughly into all the relations here involved, the Grand Duke could but be convinced that his recommendation would not attain the object hoped for by Herr Richard Wagner, at a moment when, as your honour will admit, other most weighty and trenchant questions claim all attention, so that none but a very limited sympathy could be awaited for the matter broached. To make a recommendation, however, without any prospect of equivalent success—this, in proper estimation of the tasks which Herr Richard

Wagner has set himself, his Royal Highness believed he
ought not to undertake.

While forwarding this message in obedience to the
Royal orders, I at like time have the honour to return to
you the letter of Herr Richard Wagner, and remain with
the assurance of my particular esteem

Your honour's
most devoted servant
VON Ungern-Sternberg.

CARLSRUHE, the 1st February 1874.

To his honour
    Herr EMIL HECKEL,
      Committee of the Richard Wagnerverein
        at Mannheim.

Our last hope remained the King of Bavaria.
Just as the German nation has to thank him for
Wagner's having been able to complete his work, so
it was he again who made possible a continuance of
the building, and later the performances themselves.

Dear good Friend Heckel,
Now sit you tight !
'Twill all come right !—

With His Majesty the thing is settled : the undertaking,
in which you play so splendidly serious a part, is assured.
Details presently ! —

— — — I knew that that would all be fruitless : my
cause requires a "sapient fool ! "—but who is foolish nowadays ?—

In great haste !
With all my heart
Your
RICHARD WAGNER.

BAYREUTH, 9. Feb. 1874.

And Zeroni ? ? Ah ha ! !

I answered forthwith :——

MANNHEIM, 11*th February* 1874.

Dear good Master,
     A greater joy, than your letter has afforded me to-day, I cannot conceive !   Three cheers for His Majesty King Ludwig the Second of Bavaria !   After so many failures, joy at last once more !   I hope you will right soon let me know the *how,* and dispose of me in any way where I can help you.—— ——

With the postscript : " You are the first, of whom we think in times of joy or sorrow for our cause," the master sent me word that the year 1875 was still contemplated for the festival ; only in case the works could not be finished by then, would the date be altered.
     The King's signature to the contract followed at the beginning of March.

Dear Friend,
     The King's signature has this moment arrived.   He accords us a credit of 100,000 thalers from his own privy-purse, to defray the immediate costs of the stage-equipment, scenery and gas-plant : during the term of credit all incoming Patronat monies are to be assigned to the Royal exchequer till all advances are repaid, down to which time the said remittances remain the property of the Royal Court-secretariate.
     Thus the contract.
     You will see that we have merely been placed in the position to proceed, but in nowise obtain a grant ; consequently that we remain as much committed, as ever, to bring about the whole undertaking through the public's sympathy.

Now I beg you in your messages and publications to act with the prudence and caution requisite for the two purposes :

(1) Of shewing that this new relief is a warrant that the undertaking will be consummated.

(2) Of not allowing folk to think there's no need of doing any more for it.

We therefore deem best, simply to state the fact that :

The most definite contracts for the speedy execution of the scenery and stage-equipment have just been placed with the painter Hoffmann in Vienna and Court-machinist Brandt.

I fancy this will be sufficient to stop all talk. For my part I will write at once to the singers of my choice, and issue orders about the orchestra; all of which will pretty soon give the thing another look.

It should please me all the more, that this affords you true delight, dear Friend, as I myself taste little of this joy, alas ! since I have been so wearied and worried by all that has gone before, that success finds me somewhat cold in the end, and mindful only of my duties.

Heartiest greetings from house to house !

Your

RICHARD WAGNER.

BAYREUTH, 5. *March* 1874.

I was the more delighted at the definitive conclusion of the contracts with Hoffmann and Brandt as a few weeks before, when he telegraphed for me to come to him, Wagner had determined to cancel the orders. In a later letter to Hoffmann he wrote : " What held me back, was the fact that I had been confidentially acquainted with the reason of the King's momentary pique against me, namely that something had been reported to him which he took

ill of me.   Luckily I was able to explain the (very
mischievous) occasion to the King in a way that
turned him *to my side* at once. . . ."

Upon my directing Wagner's notice to the tenor
Georg Unger and his somewhat unequal achievements as Lohengrin and Tannhäuser at the Mannheim Court-theatre, he answered :—

> Best Friend,
>   Finest thanks !—Just now we are burdened with
> the equipment of our house and approaching removal into
> it.   My wife suffering from a very obstinate cold, and I—
> awaiting good times and putting up with bad.   At the
> beginning of May I expect Richter, to help me for 4
> months.   He shall then have a look at your tenor as well.
> — — — For men I shan't lack,—of ladies I haven't many
> to boast.   The summer will clear it all up : for the mo-
> ment I still have something of the winter in my limbs ! !—
> Heartiest greetings to you and our friends from
> Yours sincerely
> RICHARD WAGNER.

BAYREUTH, 17. *April* '74.

Wagner's enemies at the Munich Court had tried
their power, as known, so early as 1864.   They
never ceased to cross his plans, in small things as in
big.   A characteristic instance is supplied by the
obduracy with which the authority concerned rejected
Wagner's application to allow him a direct entrance
from his garden into the public Hofgarten.   In
May 1873, when the King begged him to express
his annual " Birthday-wish," the master asked the
King himself to permit him to break a gap in the

hedge which divided his property from the Hof-garten, just large enough for him to slip through on his way towards the " Festspielhaus." The King's consent was given at once. This is the history of the simple little wicket-gate now opened every year at midday, during the Festival season, that guests may visit the master's sequestered grave.

On the first of September 1874 I attended with Dr. Zeroni a *Tristan* performance under Hans von Bülow in Munich. We returned viâ Bayreuth, and gave Wagner our report on the performance. It surprised him that the performers, too, had fully satisfied us. He told us of the never to be forgotten *Schnorr* and his matchless impersonation of Tristan. Wagner sang and played us the great scene for Tristan in the third act, most affectingly, to shew us how it should be rendered. It delighted him that the work had moved us so powerfully, and that our enthusiasm had led to our paying him a visit. We passed two glorious days at Bayreuth.

On the 6th December 1874 Frau Wagner in-formed me that *Götterdämmerung* was now at last completed.

At the end of the year Wagner wrote me a friendly private letter, which was followed in the new year by a number of epistolary communications con-cerning the undertaking. The latter were mainly occasioned by my share in the choice of various per-formers.

My dear Friend,

In order that I may really close the old year with something pleasant, I answer you immediately after receipt of your kind good greeting!

You dear Righteous, all of you, and especially our Joint Head-righteous Zeroni! Accept the heartiest wishes from me and mine!

Health, spirits, fun—in short—what people call the gifts of God and Nature—are good. Here and there a little hanging and throttling, but—always with the best intent.

Beautiful, quite beautiful, was your kind visit, you two Chief-righteous!—Only, bring the Mesdames Righteous with you next time!—

You shall soon have all particulars about the progress of our preparations.—

A good year to you, is the first wish of
Your
trusty
RICHARD WAGNER.

BAYREUTH, 31. *Dec.* 1874, *evening.*

Dear Friend,

Once more: a happy new year!—But now comes business: namely the details for the casting of certain parts in my thing. As I have a whole assemblage of notes of interrogation before me at Mannheim, I address myself to you as diplomat, hoping you will behave better to me than Count Arnim to Bismarck.

1. Herr Unger[1] must try to get *Loge* perfect, and besides study *Sigmund* (for an emergency); which may be of use to him in the future, if he attends all the rehearsals here, even should he not sing it at Bayreuth just yet.—

2. Herr Knapp,[2] for many of his qualities, I would

---

[1] Hans Richter had tried him at Mannheim, and recommended him.
[2] Barytone at the Mannheim Court-theatre.

gladly have for *Fafner :* friend Langer must please see if this will suit Knapp's voice (there being a few deep notes). —If *not*, let him keep to *Donner*, with the understudy of *Gunther*,—just as with Unger and Sigmund.—

3. Fräulein Auguste v. Müller : [1]

"*Grimmgerde*," one of the Walküren. *Erda*, and First Norn as understudy, *vide :* Unger-Sigmund.

4. Fräul. Johanna König [1]—the *Bird's voice* in Siegfried —the lady's somewhat diminutive figure prevents my giving her anything beyond. To be sure, I might have employed her as First Rhine-daughter "Woglinde," but I require for that, in the first rank, experienced and plucky ladies with great knowledge of the stage, as they mostly have to sing in flying-machines ; for which the Sisters Lehmann have offered me their services. *But :* prudence here, as well, is good ; Frl. König may learn *Woglinde*, and Frl. von Müller *Flosshilde* also.

Friend Langer might see to all practice.—

These the provisional combinations ; if I hear good news from you concerning the readiness of those just named, it will be followed on my side by the official measures, sending of parts, preciser settlements. But I must be perfectly assured on the point which I have calculated in my proposals, that of the *most unconditional* willingness to co-operate and abide in every way by what I deem expedient for the whole. *Singer's - touchinesses*, coveting of rôles and claims in this respect, wherever found, will compel me to break off engagements at once. Only from the free good-will of *every co-operator* can that proceed, and succeed, which I intend.

I still lack a *Sieglinde ;* worse luck ! She must be slim and presentable. Fr. Jaide will not do. Have you anything to suggest ? In case Knapp refuses Fafner, have you

---

[1] Pupil of Ernst Frank.

perhaps a decent chap for it ?   In any case it must be a really powerful deep bass.—

A thousand hearty greetings from house to house, and to the excellent Righteous !

Your

old little

RICHARD WAGNER.

BAYREUTH, 2. *Jan.* 1875.

As Knapp's voice was not deep enough for Fafner, I recommended Herr von Reichenberg.

(Post-card.)

In a few days' time official documents go out to everybody, explaining all, and—inquiring. H. v. Reichenberg shall be welcome. If you think him competent for *Fafner*, I would gladly have him here for a day or two at once.

With hearty greeting,

Your

R. W.

BAYREUTH, 14. *Jan.* '75.

Dear good Friend Heckel,

After this sheaf of provisions, one word to yourself ! So !—

Lo here the ceremonial papers, which, for reason of their high solemnity, I beg you to consign to the various parties in person. (You might even propose a toast at the time !) Commit to everyone the part allotted him. To Frl. v. Müller I have added a few words in writing, as touching " Erda," whom I do not now entrust to her alone.—However, you already know everything from my last letter, in accordance wherewith you will distribute the parts.

To Herr Knapp I can only give out, for the present, his *unconditional* part—Donner, as *Gunther* (to be studied also

To Emil Heckel 75

by him, for reasons of prudence) is not yet quite engraved. Beyond this, however, Herr Knapp must also take over 1 clansman in the Götterdämmerung for me ; all soloists, not otherwise engaged in it, take one of the 16 clansmen. Be so kind as to explain this to Herr Unger too. Everybody must be not only good—but good-natured. The clansmen's parts will follow. Herr Unger shall also receive a Sigmund-part (as understudy), but *Loge* will give him quite enough to do for the moment. If he can get away, I should be glad to hear him through it. At the end of March I shall be back in Bayreuth.—

And now, many and still other many hearty greetings from Wahnfried, from many, and also from

Your
much obliged
RICHARD WAGNER.

BAYREUTH, 25. *Jan.* 1875.

The above letter was accompanied by printed intimations from Wagner to the co-operators. I asked him about the allowance to the performers for board and lodging, and at like time begged him to send me a copy of the circular letter. I received it with the following lines on its last page :

BAYREUTH, 28. *Jan.* 1875.

Here's what you wished. 8 to 10 marks per day etc. will probably be ample for all the expenses of the less flourishing : so—tell the people they may bargain for that. Every care will be taken to provide good and *cheap* accommodation for my little troop.

Good night, dear friend !
Your
R. WAGNER.
(Chancellor.)

As the members of the Mannheim Court-theatre had to make certain contributions to its Pension-fund whenever they accepted starring engagements, Knapp demanded a higher allowance.

Dear Friend,
        To you—therefore short and resolute, as usual.
Knapp rather wearies me with his somewhat absurdly worded clause about certain additional payments. Eilers and other excellent artists, besides poor Unger, accept the simple reimbursement ; Eilers, in fact, with only ninety dollars a month. Eilers sings two principal parts for me, whereas I count definitely on nothing but Donner from Knapp, and even for that part I can get Degele of Dresden gratis. If Herr Knapp insists on his 15 marks, I shall want him only for the first week of July and the first week of August *this year*, and next year for the first half of June and from July 15 to August 21 ; he can fill up the intervals by earning money elsewhere. Candidly, this chaffering annoys me !—
        To Unger, Frl. König and Frl. von Müller I am writing myself.—Else, much goes well ; great emulation everywhere to ease me on the point of costs.
        Richter just here on his honeymoon. The 11th inst. we start ourselves for Pesth and Vienna. You ought to come to Vienna for the performance on the evening of March 1 (lots of Götterdämmerung) !
            Hearty greetings from house to house !
                    Ever and entirely
                        Your
                            RICH. WAGNER.
BAYREUTH, 6. *Feb.* 1875.

Dear Friend,
        I'm sorry for Seidel's sake that you are not Stadtrath [town-councillor] as he swore you were.

Have you no other handsome, slim, tall lady ?

We go first to Vienna, and then—perhaps—on to Pesth. We start on the 20th, and in Vienna shall stop at Standthartner's, in the Town-infirmary. I'm afraid you could only get a room there as town-patient. Rehearsals and concert are free to you—of course. In return, however, you must call out *da capo* for *one* number. I'll tell you which.

Knapp is snap !—

Best greetings to and fro !

Your

RICHARD WAGNER.

Stadtrath.

BAYREUTH, 9. *Feb.* 1875.

Dear Friend Heckel,

As (what I should not have expected) you have textually imparted to Herr Knapp my last letter concerning him, and thus placed him in the predicament of applying to himself certain confidential, almost jocular expressions,— I now beg you to make him textually acquainted with this communication of to-day as well.

I entirely absolve Herr Knapp from any suspicion of seeking personal profit from a certain regulation of the Mannheim Court-theatre : I prize his person and his talent ; and I declare that, if I felt myself authorised to assist an artist at the expense of my Patrons, I should not have a moment's hesitation in according Herr Knapp the amplest allowance. Only, I here encounter a decision of the Mannheim Theatre-committee which absolutely staggers me. To impose on an artist, who profits nothing by this occasion, a tribute such as can only be claimed from a personal gain—and this in view of an undertaking such as mine, where everything is brought to pass by free-willed sacrifice—betrays an aim and sentiment which make me long to see them publicly chastised.

My Patrons shall *not* pay this precious Committee their tribute, and so I renounce, and solely upon *this* ground, the co-operation of our highly-honoured friend Herr Knapp in my Festspiels.—

With heartiest greeting I remain
Your
RICHARD WAGNER.

BAYREUTH, 13. *February* 1875.

My next question Wagner answered at first by a telegram :

Emil Heckel, Mannheim.

If Reichenberg deep bass, Fafner, let him come to-morrow. If not, journey aimless. Viennese departure Sunday.
Wagner.

Dear Friend Heckel,
      Many thanks !—Much toil and trouble.—I would gladly see Herr v. Reichenberg, but my time is now scant (*knapp*), which brings me to the prayer that you would put things straight with Herr Knapp.   Since the Herren Kapellmeister behave so badly, I've become tired of higgling and haggling.   But Knapp really interests me.   Let him but arrange his time well, according to the order of rehearsals, i.e. *I* need him only for the Rheingold, and—if he will sing a Clansman—for Götterdämmerung ; during the other pieces he is welcome to star for himself and so on, nor would I willingly pay for the time when he lies idle here, especially to benefit the Mannheim pension fund.—
      As regards Herr Unger, at this moment I'm still most uncertain about it.   You know that !
      I am awaiting news, according to which I hope to see Tristan in Munich by April the 5th at latest : if *Frau Vogel* comes up to my wishes, and if I can secure her for

Sieglinde, there's little doubt but that I shall have to take her husband also. Now, I have no other part to offer him, save *Loge*. In that case I shouldn't quite know what to do with Herr Unger, whom as yet I know so little. Nevertheless the latter has left with me a memory which moves me—*in any case*—to make his closer acquaintance. For that purpose he would have to spend a little time in my vicinity, were it merely for sake of learning from me something useful to himself. Only, I can pay him no keep.

Just see what can be managed in the matter.

In the event of Frau Vogel's definitively dissatisfying me, Unger would certainly appear as *Loge*.

I've lately gone through a deal of racket, and also am not well. But everything must come right in the end.

Hearty greeting from
Your
trusty
RICHARD WAGNER.

BAYREUTH, 26*th March* 1875.

Reichenberg would certainly find me at Bayreuth from now till the first day or two in April.

Dear Friend,

Many thanks for Herr v. Reichenberg: he's a decided acquisition, both for now and the future.—

Who recommended you the two lady singers at Bremen? I might perhaps get one of them to come to Hanover, where I shall be stopping on Sunday and Monday—the 11th and 12th April—for sake of the tenor. Could you effect some such thing?—

The accounts which Reichenberg gave me of Unger, as concerns his voice, were not favourable; if he cannot keep to a single note, I can never teach it him. I'm getting afraid of him. — — —

I wish for Knapp in any case.—Berlin concert—24th
April:—God knows!—
Best greetings from your
RICHARD WAGNER.

BAYREUTH, 2nd April 1875.

Most honoured Friend,
        Do but send me Herr Unger! I've a good idea
regarding him, especially for himself. If I see that there's
anything to be done with him, I shall teach him the
Tannhäuser for Vienna, where he then might get engaged.
Right!—
    Is it all over with Knapp then?
    I'm sorry.—
    Patronise well! We are badly off, and I hardly know
where to procure the money for this year's rehearsals!
Everything costs more than was anticipated, and Runck-
witz [the builder] devours all!—
Hearty greetings!
Your
RICH. WAGNER.

BAYREUTH, 10. May 1875.

    On the 22nd May we sent the master our
birthday congratulations.   He replied:

Best thanks to all
Righteouses and Righteousesses!
    My good wife rejoiced me with a splendid garden-treat
on my birthday!
But: — —
business!—
    Unger has never come, though I telegraphed him twice
about important prospects. I suppose I shall have to give
him up as well, already. — — —

To Emil Heckel 81

Forgive me! Your little questions about so-and-so, whether he might attend rehearsals? . . . and so on, often demand answers that do not come so easy to me,—for I'm much more bothered than you seem to think. The preliminary *lessons*, not rehearsals, of this year are intended purely for the thing, not for the listener : from the 1st to the 15th August, however, there will be orchestral rehearsals, for position, seating, sound, first reading. Who happens to be there, and behaves himself discreetly, will perhaps find something to hear in the end ; but special *permits* will not go out.—

What difficulties I still have before me !—

If the Righteous would only realise that, and not be always congratulating me in advance on my "successes" !—

Many hearty greetings,

Your

R. WAGNER.

BAYREUTH, 27. *May* 1875.

I had complied with Wagner's invitation, in his letter of February 6, to come to Vienna. The concert-performances of portions of *Götterdämmerung* went off magnificently. Materna, as Brünnhilde, already roused our highest expectations, whereas Glatz of Pesth did not prove equal to the part of Siegfried.

Wagner stayed with the Standhartners. At their house he sang us one evening the whole third act of *Götterdämmerung*, Joseph Rubinstein accompanying on the pianoforte. It was overpowering, the expression with which the master rendered everything ; lucky those who were favoured to listen ! Beyond Frau Wagner and the Standhartners, only Countess

G

von Dönhof, Anton Bruckner and myself were present.

Wagner prized Bruckner very highly, and spoke of performing his symphonies, which had then found understanding nowhere. The master also made the acquaintance of another Viennese composer in those days : Hugo Wolf, to whom we owe the newer German Lied, paid him a visit, the young man laying his first-fruits before the elder.

At supper, Wagner proposed the following health to Captain Schönaich, Standhartner's stepson, who had just recovered from a serious illness :

> " Come, spruce my Captain, hold your stand !
> Indeed it is an utter scand-
> -al that your good father Stand-
> -hartner could lay no healing hand.
> Now that the malady is past,
> the remedy is found at last ;
> yestreen I gave a little clinking,
> to-night your health we'll all be drinking :
> Live happily, and live you long,
> to teach old Death that he eyed wrong ! "

On March the 3rd a grand festivity took place in Hans Makart's gorgeous studio, in honour of Wagner. Besides the higher aristocracy, almost everyone of note in Art and Science was present. The fête went off most brilliantly. The ladies vied with one another to prove their taste to Makart by the choicest of toilets. He was an admirable host.

The Helmesberger Quartet played Beethoven. When somebody sat down to the piano, and began

to improvise on Wagner's works, the master seized
me by the arm and said : " Come along, Heckel ;
let's go into the other room. I can't have people
playing my own things to me."

In course of the evening, when a well-known poet
and successful dramatist came up to us, and remarked
that the German public had never yet come forward
to a great contemporary as it had to Wagner, the
latter humorously replied : " Eh ! the *Sultan* and
the *Khedive of Egypt* took patronat-vouchers," then,
turning to Semper, who had just come up : " I know
but a few who have worked and still work in earnest
for the cause. These are Frau von Schleinitz in
Berlin, Countess von Dönhof in Vienna, and there
my Heckel " (rapping me on the shoulder), " who
plucks the people on another side. While the others
labour from above downwards, Heckel is working
from below up."

*   *

*

In a letter to the master I mentioned that Brahms
intended coming to Mannheim and Heidelberg. In
answer, Wagner wrote me :

Dear Friend,
        Please find out where Brahms puts up, and let him
have this letter.
Everything goes fairly forward. Soon more !
                Yours faithfully,
                        RICHARD WAGNER.
BAYREUTH, 6. *June* 1875.

Brahms was in possession of a manuscript of Wagner's, which the latter begged back, sending Brahms a score of the *Rheingold* in exchange.

The letter above-mentioned reached Brahms at Ziegelhausen, near Heidelberg, from which place he acquainted me with its receipt. He paid me a call in Mannheim, when, as also on my return call at Ziegelhausen, we discussed the Bayreuth undertaking. However, I derived the impression that Brahms was not displeased that Wagner's opponents should play him off as antagonist of the Bayreuth master.

Concerning various instant questions with regard to the undertaking, and particularly the hotel which Albert of Heidelberg desired to build at Bayreuth for the festivals, I corresponded chiefly with Frau Wagner.

When I heard that Unger, who originally was to sing the part of Loge, had been entrusted with that of Siegfried, I doubted his capacity. Wagner replied to me as follows :

Eh ! Eh ! Friend Heckel ! Your verdict veers so easily ? A little while back you were all for Unger,—to-day you put your faith in Jäger !—Now I am in with Unger ; to be sure, I've had a heap of trouble in overcoming his Saxon vocalism, which completely masked his voice, but I now have hopes that I shall get on better with him than with any other tenor of my acquaintance. And I shall keep him tied here ; he was obviously a lost, but not an unenergetic creature. Jäger is excellent, but — — —

The question of accommodation here now enters a

new phase ; we shall have to do without building a new hotel.

Hearty greeting from

Your
trusty composer
R. WAGNER.

BAYREUTH, 25. *June* 1875.

What is Frl. v. Müller's exact address ?

On the 30th July 1875 I set out for Bayreuth, with my wife, to attend the practice and rehearsals. We remained until August 17. It was a time immensely rich in deep impressions, but also in cares and agitations.

If even in ordinary stage relations one's commerce with the impersonating artists demands an intuitive understanding of their quick susceptibility, here, where so infinitely much depended on the good will of every individual, the height of tact was requisite, to bring about harmonious co-ordination without draconic laws. Any want of insight, any pedantic construing of words that merely sprang from spontaneous impulse without reflection, would here have led to fatal trouble. The extraordinary character of the undertaking, not to be dealt with in the usual way at all, bore in itself a crop of seeds for rapid generation of misunderstandings.

As so much often hung on the immediate smoothing out of unexpected wrinkles, I went daily to the office of the Verwaltungsrath at Banker Feustel's the first thing in the morning, acquainted myself with everything that had occurred, and then made my call upon Wagner. I would mostly find him in the garden, taking coffee with his wife and Liszt. The first question generally ran : " Is no one leaving ? " for the threat to " go away at once " was a standing refrain to every declaration of the grumblers.

In parleys with the artists Frau Wagner did her utmost, with a self-sacrifice beyond all praise, to settle all unpleasantnesses in the master's stead. In Wagner's personal behaviour toward his artists there often reigned unbounded jollity. At the last pianoforte-rehearsal in the Hotel Sonne he literally stood upon his head for very glee. In view of the fatigue entailed on many by the unwonted style of his work, he always strove to keep them in good humour, and laid great stress on the community of toil and object.

Before evening he would generally look in at " Angermann's." It was not merely recreation, that he sought here in the circle of his artists ; he wished to preserve a personal connection with them ; they were to learn to understand both him and his artistic aims. The evenings at Wahnfried, having more a social character, could not lend themselves so well to easy interchange of views, as this informal comradeship at Angermann's. The house, most simple at that time, acquired through Wagner a world-celebrity.

Wagner had the highest gift of entering into every artistic individuality. Little as he would make concessions to operatic wont and stage-conventions, he was always anxious that each performer should fulfil

his task in his natural fashion. I remember his
shewing Niemann how to do a scene in the second
act of *Die Walküre*. When the singer replied :
" Dear master, that suits your figure very well, but
doesn't mine. With my size, I must make gestures
in keeping ! "—Wagner agreed at once, and said :
" I see, you understand me ; that was the only
question. Now act it how you yourself think best."
That the performance suffered nothing in unity of
style, however, through indulgence of whims or
wilful eccentricities, was ensured by the creative
charm that flowed from Wagner, and by his genius
as scenist. A few characteristic hints would often
suffice to prompt individual talents to strike a path
in full accordance with the spirit of his work.

Every night from 8 to 10 o'clock there was a
social gathering at Wahnfried ; for Wagner felt at
home in the midst of his friends and artists. If the
weather was fine, we would stroll into the garden ;
but if *Liszt* sat down at the piano, we all rushed
back indoors. Those who never heard him, even if
they have known Bülow, Rubinstein or Tausig, can
form no idea of the indescribable magic of his touch.
He would often lend a work so personal a poetic
charm, that one could feel in it that tenderness we
know so well from his delightful Correspondence
with Wagner. And if fair ladies sat around him,
his playing almost took the character of a fascinating
tête-à-tête. He no longer seemed to be reproducing
a work, but immediately expressing, as it were, what
once had found an utterance therein. His playing

no more seemed the rendering of a pianoforte-piece, but artistic conversation: the conversation of a Liszt! Perhaps if his own works were interpreted in this sense, they might be understood more readily.

In after years I often heard Liszt play again in an intimate circle, alike at Bayreuth as at Freiburg im Breisgau, where he attended the excellent performance of his *Christus* under Dimmler, and at Baden-Baden.   Once—outside the Festspiel season—he played some new compositions of his at Wahnfried, among them the wonderful "Vogelpredigt."   Then, after discussing with Liszt the rendering of a fugue of Bach's from the "Wohltemperirtes Klavier," Wagner played it with convincing emphasis on his particular reading.   Beyond the family, only Frau von Meyendorf from Weimar, my wife and myself, were present.   Wagner and Liszt fell reminding each other of the best waltzes written at the time of their youth.   Liszt played from memory those of Strauss, and Wagner those of Lanner.   We danced to them.   "Herr Heckel," said Frau von Meyendorf, "never have I danced to such good playing. Wagner and Liszt as dance-musicians!"   The word was taken up by both the masters, and unforced gaiety prevailed the evening long.

With Wagner's invitation to remove from Mannheim to Bayreuth for good, I could not comply, on account of my business ; yet Bayreuth became my second home.

Liszt knew of the wars I had had to wage against the musical reactionaries at Mannheim, and in still later

years, upon my visiting him at Weimar, he asked me with
relation to the former Handel-performances: "Well,
is there as much Halleluja singing in Mannheim as
ever?" Fortunately I could answer in the negative,
and a little while after, when I had the privilege of
welcoming him to my own house at Mannheim, our
performance of *Götterdämmerung* convinced him that
the times and the "Wagnerianer" had brought a
certain change about.

During the stage-rehearsals I was much assisted
by the "Leitmotive" extracted from *Rheingold* and
Walküre by Federlein of Munich (now in America).
I had cut them out of the *Musikalisches Wochenblatt*,
and pasted them in corresponding places in my text-
book. This collection much interested Liszt: so early
as the performances of *Tannhäuser* and *Lohengrin* at
Weimar he had drawn attention to the Leitmotive
of these works in his preparatory comments. I
proposed to Hans von Wolzogen to continue
Federlein's work by gathering the motives from
Siegfried and *Götterdämmerung* also; after discussing
the matter with Liszt, he agreed, and extended his
labours to the whole four sections of the drama.
Thus arose his well-known "Thematischer Leitfaden
durch die Musik des 'Ring des Nibelungen,'" since
followed by many another.

After the rehearsals were over, I left Bayreuth, rich
in powerful impressions, but not without anxieties
about the financial basis of the undertaking, for
contributions were scanty.

In memory of this period Wagner presented me

with a copper medallion bearing his portrait by
Scharff of Vienna. Upon a circular to the artists,
which I had begged the master to send on to me, he
wrote the words :

> Most excellent of all Patron-mongers !
> By the way, things are going just so-so !—
> A Cantor Fischer of Zwickau lately caught me 6⅔
> Patrons, sent me 6000 marks, and asked if he might have a
> free seat for it. (! ! !)—
> 21st inst. Tannhäuser here.
> —(! !)—
> I have no lists of rehearsals at hand ; get one sent you
> by Feustel, or Fischer (Nibelungen-treasury).
> > Many hearty greetings from
> > > Your fagged out
> > > > RICHARD WAGNER.
> VIENNA, 11. *Nov.* '75.

Bad news from Feustel, about the deficiency of
funds, were confirmed by Wagner's ensuing letter :

> Dearest best Friend,
> To the question, "How goes't with us ?" there
> would be much to answer. The world, and in particular
> "Germania," grows more and more obnoxious to me !
> Our anxieties are great, and I've come to the conclusion
> that it is raving madness to let the performances take place
> this year. Our Patronat-vouchers have reached 490 ; but,
> according to the latest computations, we need 1300 to pull
> us through. The originally projected undertaking is there-
> fore, strictly speaking, wrecked. Now we must have the
> impudence to see what Curiosity will bring us. Even
> Feustel believes we may run the risk ; only, we are faced
> with a dearth of money in June, when the bandsmen and

singers arrive and will want hard cash. I have begged for an advance of 30,000 thlr. from the Kaiser. I shall see what can be done when I go to Berlin at the beginning of March,—to see again, in another light, how things stand there with "Tristan," neither in which do I quite believe as yet.—For the rest, we keep a good appearance here. Everything is getting ready (on credit!); the artistic details of the execution are being worked out to the highest perfection. Brandt, as ever, firstrate,—my pillar of strength!

I have had no unpleasantness from any of the singers save X.: everyone seems to stick to the thing with dauntless courage. X. I shall be able to replace,—even if he doesn't come round at the last minute; it's not quite over with him yet. Otherwise little new.

Greet wife and friends sincerely from me and us!

If you can conjure up anything, I shall be delighted! Always, however, I remain

Your

most cordially devoted

RICHARD WAGNER.

BAYREUTH, 4. *Feb.* 1876.

March 12, 1876, I went to Bayreuth for a conference with the Verwaltungsrath. Thence to Berlin —whither Wagner had already departed—for the representation of *Tristan und Isolde.* After the performance Kaiser Wilhelm I. most heartily expressed his admiration to Wagner, and promised to come to Bayreuth for the first performance of the Bühnenfestspiel. Wagner told me that the King of Bavaria had already placed his palaces in Bayreuth at the Kaiser's disposal, and would himself arrive for the dress-rehearsals.

As I was stopping at the same hotel as Wagner, the "Thiergarten," he referred all interviewers to me.

One evening, after Joseph Rubinstein had played us Wagner's "American March" (written for the Centenary of the Declaration of Independence), the master said he had received a very handsome fee for it. Then, drawing a five-cent piece from his waist-coat-pocket, he gave it me : "There Heckel, I've *this* still left from the honorarium, and present it you. Feustel has already spent all the rest."

On the 22nd March I took leave of Wagner and his wife, engaging to arrive at Bayreuth in good time for the festivals.

*   *

*

So long ago as the last autumn, Wagner had made an announcement in the *Musikalisches Wochenblatt*, directing all who wished for free admission to the festivals to apply to the Wagnervereins, and to that of Mannheim in especial. However, it was not until April 1876, that he published definite particulars about the distribution, with which he acquainted me beforehand in the following lines :

Dearest Friend,
    In a few days' time an announcement about the free seats will appear, which will certainly delight you in the highest measure.
                    Heartiest greeting.
                            Your
                            RICHARD WAGNER.

8. *April '76.*

Unfortunately the number of free places had afterwards to be diminished, as certain structural alterations put an end to a number of seats.

In the first half of 1876 our correspondence by letter was rarer, as I returned to Bayreuth by the 14th of May, this time for a meeting of delegates from the Wagnervereins and Patrons. At the master's request, Adolph Gross, of Bayreuth, and myself joined the " Verwaltungsrath."

After my arrival home again on the 17th, I sent Wagner my birthday-congratulation, followed on the 22nd by the yearly complimentary telegram from the " Mannheim Righteous." On the 22nd May, 1813, was Wagner born ; the 22nd May, 1831, was my own day of birth. This coincidence was emphasised by the 22nd May, 1871, being the day on which I proposed to Tausig in Berlin the foundation of Wagnervereins.

On Wagner's behalf I received an invitation to attend all the performances of the Bühnenfestspiel " as honorary Patron." On July 9, accordingly, I set out with my wife for two months at Bayreuth, to witness the fulfilment of an enterprise whose furtherance for years had formed the voluntary goal of my endeavours, and usurped my inmost thought and feeling.

* *

*

The load of work that fell to the Verwaltungsrath both before and during the Festspiels was no light

one, and Wagner greeted my arrival with the words :
"You've come at last!"   Again, as in 1875, we
had to settle many awkward differences ; but the
power of genius, obeyed by everybody in the end,
held all together.   The grandeur of the artwork,
and the consciousness of contributing their quota to
its living realisation, shed on all concerned a spell
that exorcised each selfish interest at the crucial
moment.

Wagner drew up various placards of notification
to the public or the performers ; the following he
sent me on the 14th August, for transmission to the
printer :

The honoured Patrons of the Bühnenfestspiels must not
take it ill of either the author or the performers, if they do
not acknowledge the marks of approbation most kindly
bestowed on them by appearing before the curtain, as they
have agreed to carry out this abnegation in order to present
themselves before the public exclusively within the frame of
the artwork represented by them.

RICHARD WAGNER.

Owing to the presence of King Ludwig of
Bavaria, the festival in reality began with the dress-
rehearsal on August 6-9.

The Kaiser came to the first performance.   At
the station, pointing to the Festspielhaus, he said to
Wagner in our hearing : "So, the sun is really
shining on your work," and confessed that he had
not believed Wagner would bring it about.

The artistic success of the three representations

was quite out of the ordinary, but I must leave
my own intense impressions unexpressed in words.
Wagner himself was highly pleased with the execution, regarded as a whole. The words he wrote
upon his photograph, which he gave me as a parting
present, sum up his verdict :

> O friend Heckel,
> It yet was good !
> RICHARD WAGNER.

BAYREUTH 1876.

King Ludwig came back for the last representation. He greeted us with kindly words, but it was
impossible for anyone save Wagner to speak with
him during the performances, as he employed each
interval in studying the poem.

Unfortunately the funds in hand proved in-
sufficient, to the last. His Bayreuth friends consequently implored Wagner to use his personal
influence with the King to obtain a fresh credit.
But Wagner refused to mar the joy which the warm
enthusiasm of his Royal friend had given him. The
feeling that in these festival days he was thanking
the King by his work, as it were, for all past favours,
made him energetically reject all importuning of the
sort, in his endeavour, as he put it, " to diminish,
not increase, his obligations toward the King."

Our accounts shewed a net deficit of about
160,000 marks [£8000], a grievous and disquieting
result. I begged the Verwaltungsrath to persuade
the town of Bayreuth to undertake the covering of a

portion of the deficit, leaving us to seek in private
ways to move the Patrons to discharge the balance.
Unhappily my repeated letters were always met by
the reply that it would be absolutely useless to
address such a request to the town : when it gave
the site for the undertaking, it had been promised
that it should in no case be drawn into any financial
involvement.

Wagner decided to send out a printed circular to
the Patrons, beseeching them to defray the deficit,
whereas the Bayreuth members of the Verwaltungsrath
continued urging him to find assistance through the
favour of his Royal friend.   On the 30th October
1876 I wrote to Wagner :

"Dear Master,
    "You of course have heard through your
Verwaltungsrath in Bayreuth, that I have declared
myself against your sending out a circular as to
covering the deficit.   It is *our* business to collect the
money, and I am of opinion that this should be done
by letters and personal visits to sterling friends.—
My first visit, to Herr Friedr. Schön at Worms,
resulted in his placing 1000 marks at my command ;
of this I have apprised Bayreuth, but as yet have
received no answer as to what has been resolved on.
I also have repeatedly written the gentlemen that,
even if the town as such can contribute nothing to
covering the deficit, at least the citizens should collect
a substantial sum among themselves.—To-day I have
come by the idea that in 1877, instead of three—

four representations might be given, the takings of the *first* to be devoted to covering the deficit; on which occasion higher voluntary contributions than 100 mk. might well be paid.—I would not have troubled you with business-worries amid the beauties of Sorrento, but my plan of welcoming you back with the news 'The deficit is covered' is again frustrated; for which we must lay a portion of the blame on 'Russians, Turks and Servians.'"

Wagner answered me in his hearty fashion:

My dearest Friend Heckel,
    You really are the first to send me a sympathetic sign of life from Germany. My thanks for it.

Herr Feustel has written me nothing, down to the present, but horrors about the growing deficit, which I alone am expected to remedy. Good! I have composed and despatched my circular; I have inquired in Berlin, and of the King of B., — without as yet receiving any answer. —Under such miserable circumstances, your idea of a 4th performance to cover the deficit is certainly the most decorous; only, people will not be able to wait so long for the payment of certain bills. Now, as I have had nothing but misery with the winding-up of my Festspiels, and I should need a very strong inducement to repeat and continue them, before I could overcome my boundless repugnance against any further concern therewith,—I really am only waiting for a crowning abomination to decide me to break up everything, and that in the most literal sense. I shall then turn absolutely silent, and hand everything there to the creditors of my undertaking without a word, exactly as with a legal bankruptcy.—

Indeed you are the only one—the only one of all, to shew a noble care about myself and the affair!—

H

My health, under such conditions, is none of the best:
my inner trouble, and the flutter of uncertainty, are too
great.   On the other hand I am rejoiced by the thriving of
my wife and children in this beautiful locality.   Yet we
shall soon have to quit Sorrento (which—facing North—is
strictly but a summer resort) : probably we shall spend from
the middle of this month to the 2nd quarter of December
in Rome, then about 14 days in Florence ; in any case
we must soon be turning home, as my very hard-put household purse (in spite of American March) will not sustain
us here much longer.

Till the 10th inst. I am here : letters will be sent after me.

So ! the very heartiest greeting from Wagners to
Heckels.

Your
very devoted
RICH. WAGNER.

SORRENTO, HÔTEL VICTORIA,
3. Nov. 1876.

To avoid any slur upon Feustel, I here must state
that in all his life Wagner's financial affairs were
probably never in better and more faithful and
unselfish hands, than in those of the head of the
Feustel banking-house.   If after the festivals he paid
less heed to the feelings which must necessarily pre-
occupy Wagner after an event so pregnant for the
future, than to the business aspect of the matter, he
was forced thereto by the serious nature of the
situation, which led one to expect immediate process
on part of the creditors.   He acquainted me with
his fears by letter, saying that my conception of the
thing might raise false hopes in Wagner's mind, as
supplementary payments by the Patrons were scarcely

to be counted on ; it therefore was the duty of all true friends of Wagner to make him fully realise the seriousness of the position, if the worst consequences were not to ensue.

I could not conceal from myself that Wagner's circular, whereof Feustel had sent me a few copies with the request to make "prudent use" of them, would only drag the thing into publicity, without reaping any success in such troublous times. Therefore I deemed it my duty not to withhold from Wagner that I recognised the justice of many of Feustel's objections. It was not until receipt of his answer that I realised how much he took the thing to heart.

Dear Friend,

That you, as well, can have the heart to give my self and plight no further thought, and merely speak to me about that affair in the same tone as my other friends, has much distressed me. No one knows what to suggest; nay, even my appeal to the Patrons is only to be sent out "with prudence," because the times are too bad, and yet the performances are to be announced again as soon as possible ! It is incredible ! You even ask about the Festival-medal, which I naturally countermanded as soon as the ever-increasing deficit was reported to me. What on earth do people expect of me ?—No : I now inform you positively, that I shall devote next summer to nothing but the possible recruiting of my health,—for which, on account of the wearing and increasing pains in my abdomen, I think of taking a very protracted course of waters at Marienbad and so on. If I find myself restored to health, we will see what can be brought to pass in the year after next. If the deficit is not covered in the interim, and that without any further labour on my side, I propose to hand the whole theatre over to some entrepreneur or other, perhaps even to the Munich Court-theatre, and never bother my head about it again.

Here, dear friend, my strength gives out. My undertaking hitherto was a question to the German public : "Do you will it ? "—Now I assume that it doesn't, and accordingly have come to end. I beg you henceforward to look at the thing in sole light of these statements, and, if you deem proper, to give my other friends — — an equally summary enlightenment about myself, whom they don't seem able to understand.

In one of my perpetually sleepless nights I have tried to gain a little ease by telling a true and sympathetic friend, as which I always have regarded you, the exact and final truth about myself.

Remain good to me !

Your
ever devoted
RICHARD WAGNER.

FLORENCE, HOTEL NEW-YORK,
    9. Dec. 1876.

Wagner's words to the public, after the first representation of the *Ring des Nibelungen* : "You have seen what we can do : *'tis now for you to will!* And if you will, we have an Art," had at once been caught up by the newspapers and (despite his after-commentary, " a new German Art ") distorted into the pettiest meaning, without any comprehending that those words were a challenge to the nation to assist in the " Festivals." The audience at the performances was brilliant enough, but, taken, as a whole, by no means that receptive body for which Wagner had hoped.

Of this I was fully aware, and I wrote the master : "Your question to the German Public I understood at once in Bayreuth, yet had to tell myself that but the fewest of those present were of that kind we had awaited." Upon Friedrich Nietzsche this disillusion with regard to the audience had so dispiriting an effect, that he left Bayreuth before the performances were over, and doubted that one ever could arrive in this way at unity of German Culture.—

Faithful to my principle of making no empty suggestions, but setting hand myself wherever possible, immediately on receipt of Wagner's letter of December 9 I wrote to Herr Hofrath von Düfflipp, Cabinet-Secretary to the King of Bavaria, stating the position of affairs and asking whether any help might be expected from the King. As Wagner had meanwhile addressed himself direct to King Ludwig, I soon received from Bayreuth the auspicious news that Herr Hofrath von Düfflipp would arrive for a consultation with Wagner.

The circular to the Patrons was not even answered by more than a handful, and the conference with Herr Düfflipp led at first to no result whatever.

About that time the King of Bavaria had allowed me to transmit to him a unique set of Alpine Flora, collected by my father on his tours. I offered Wagner to attempt, if he considered fit, to obtain an audience of the King, and acquaint him with the troubles of the undertaking. The master answered:

O dearest, dearest Friend !

Yes, yes ! The King of Bavaria ! ! As if there were

any omission of *mine* to be repaired there !—Don't you think that if anybody could do something in that quarter, it would be myself; and do you fancy I've not done my uttermost? Please say no more about it !—

Yet you surely must have seen, dear friend, that all that I have started now has merely been to save the honour of my undertaking and my own position toward it.   Do you believe that I really entertain the hope of anything coming to pass?   Learn to know Germany and the German public! There everything—all is lost !—Believe me !

What we brought about last year was a miracle, and will remain so, as long as anyone remembers it.   But beyond that we can go no longer : that we must recognise.

Performances this year have already become impossible, for inner and outer reasons ; no amount of money would now accomplish anything ; for the inner damage is the worse.   The idea of a resumption could only be entertained if my programme of a Patronatverein etc. (but not on the mere basis of the former sweepstake-clubs) were strictly carried out and realised.   The new would have to wear another look than the old ; power and consciousness would have to be there.

Meanwhile I have to care for covering the deficit : I therefore think of giving concerts in England for a couple of months, solely for this purpose.   If I come back whole, I hope that nobody will any longer ask me to think of anything but—recovering—and forgetting—myself !—

Thus far have we got !—

So, best friend, put His Majesty of Bavaria out of your head, and remain good to

Your
always friendlily devoted
RICH. WAGNER.

BAYREUTH, 11. *Feb.* '77.

During the festivals the master had already discussed with Hans Richter and myself his intention of forming a *Patronatverein*, whose members alone should have the right of entry to future Festspiels. It was proposed in this way to provide a financial basis, on the one hand, on the other to exclude the public that merely took seats at the last moment out of idle curiosity or hostile intent. In January 1877 Wagner issued a circular to all the committees of Wagnervereins,[1] with the object of founding such a Patronatverein; at Easter, accordingly, an assembly of delegates was held in Leipzig. I attended the debates, at the master's particular request, as the Leipzig convokers were scheming for a transference of the festivals to their own city. After protracted efforts, I succeeded in defeating this project and getting certain resolutions passed which I had previously discussed with the master at Bayreuth. To my epistolary report of the proceedings he replied in few but characteristic lines:

My dear Heckel,
God grant you long life, at anyrate a good deal longer than my own, that there may be somebody, after my death, to form a stock—in himself—for further planting!
I understand all, but say little now; wherever possible, nothing. I can do no else than wait until outsiders catch me up, for I seem to have stridden too far ahead!
Hearty greeting!
Your
RICH. WAGNER.

BAYREUTH, 11. *Apr.* 1877.

---

[1] See *Prose Works*, vi. 15.—TR.

104 Letters of Richard Wagner

In May he went to London, to conduct the concerts there arranged for by Wilhelmj. To us Germans it is an eternal disgrace, that Wagner should have been forced to this step, to cover the deficit on a national undertaking.

Partly through the profits of the London concerts [inconsiderable.—Tr.], and partly through contributions placed at his command, such as the receipts of Hans von Bülow's concerts for the benefit of Bayreuth, it became possible to settle the most pressing debts. A fine example of self-sacrifice was set by Glasenapp, who for this purpose handed me the fee for his admirable biography of Wagner; also by a Herr Adolf Schmidt of Viersen, who placed his name at the head of a subscription-list of Patrons.

However, the main requirements could only be met by aid of the King of Bavaria. The previous advances made by the royal Privy Purse had already been repaid by the yield of our patronat-vouchers. To cover the deficit on the Festspiels themselves a sum was borrowed through the Feustel bank from an outer banking-house, under guarantee of the King's Privy Purse, to refund which the tantièmes payable by the Munich Court-theatre to Wagner were set aside.

*　　*

*

After his return from London, Wagner stayed awhile at Ems; his wretched experiences and the fatigues of the concerts had made him look quite ill, as may be seen even from the photographs taken in England, which I received through Frau Wagner's kindness. I called upon him on June the 22nd, 1877. His first greeting was a loud complaint that he should again be reminded of the miserable state of finances, and compelled to speak about it ; but as soon as he had given vent to his spleen, he expressed his delight at my visit. He was living most retiredly at Ems. On the promenade, upon seeing a little gentleman approach us, he said : "I now will present you to my only society in Ems." It was Wind-horst.

In July I met Wagner at Heidelberg. I received him at the station, upon his arrival from Ems. His health was re-established ; his spirits, for the most part, of the best. When a Heidelberg singing-club serenaded him, under Langer, he returned thanks by joining in the "Gaudeamus." Generally I spent the evening with him at the Schloss-hotel, but returned at night to Mannheim, no great distance.

On July 7 Wagner telegraphed me :

Please bring Zeroni to dine with us at 1 *to-morrow.*
Evening reading of Parsifal,[1] *to which invite the parson also.*
Wagner.

Besides Zeroni, myself, and the Old-Catholic pastor Friedrich Bauer of Mannheim, an enthusiastic admirer of the master, Richard Pohl also came, from

---

[1] It had already been read aloud by Wagner at Mr. Edward Dannreuther's house in London, May 1877.—Tr.

Baden. We were the first in Germany to make acquaintance with Wagner's poem of *Parsifal*. The expression and profound emotion, with which the master read it out to us, are indescribable. He himself was so moved, that he withdrew for awhile when the reading was over, and left us alone. But we too remained in silence, and it was long before we found ourselves back on the common earth.

At supper Wagner drank my health, in a toast which he ended with the words :

> " The soul now soars to top o' tree :
> Our Heckel joins the Committee ! "

Hotel-keeper Albert had betrayed to him my intention of getting myself elected to the Committee of the Mannheim Court-theatre.

On July 13, Wagner rejoiced me by his visit to Mannheim. In September he invited me to a " meeting of delegates " at Bayreuth, and referred in his letter to the position of President of the Committee of the Mannheim Court-theatre upon which I had entered meanwhile.

Dear Friend,
Great Theatre-director !
It occurs to me that you may have been surprised at my not addressing my invitation to a meeting of my Patrons to yourself in the first place.—

Let us hope you understand that my regard for your very difficult present position at Mannheim was my only reason. In fact I shall quite comprehend, if you don't come to Bayreuth *at all*, since none can judge better than myself

To Emil Heckel 107

what a load you have bound to your neck with this Mannheim theatre. If you come to Bayreuth *nevertheless*, rest assured that I shall call no one more welcome here, than— my dear, good friend Heckel !

Best greetings from
Yours sincerely
Richard Wagner.

Bayreuth, 9. *Sept.* 1877.

I attended the meetings at Bayreuth on the 15th and 16th of September. They were followed by the definitive foundation of the "Patronatverein," which was also to be part-owner of the "Stylbildungsschule" [School of Style] whose conduct Wagner wished to undertake. I possess the manuscript of a written communication of Wagner's to the delegates which was not published at the time :[1]

Position of the Patronat-Verein towards the project mooted.

The Patronat-Verein is aware of the goal, and resolves to employ its contributions for attainment thereof. This is facilitated by the fact that the costs of the undertaking will become considerable only in course of time, but for the first few years lesser means will suffice ; whereas it is to be assumed that, if everything goes well, the support afforded us will constantly increase.

The cost of setting up the School I estimate at 10,000 marks [£500] per annum ; the town of Bayreuth displays its willingness to bear a portion thereof. Consequently the Patronatverein would have to devote its monetary collections to a standing fund, and entrust the administration of the same to a Verwaltungsrath at Bayreuth.

---

[1] First printed in Karl Heckel's "Bie Bühnenfestspiele in Bayreuth," pp. 57-58. For the Prospectus of September 15, 1877, see *Prose Works*, vi. 19.—Tr.

The Patronatverein is an active partner in the School ; its members enjoy the School - instruction gratis ; consequently nothing qualifies for a share in that instruction, saving membership of the Patronatverein.

Admission to the public performances in the summer months, as also to the later scenic representations themselves, likewise gratis, is open to none but members of the Patronatverein.—

With the whole series of performances in the year 1883 the Bühnenfestspiels are finally established, and will be repeated every year as models.   To the Patronatverein belongs for all time the care of maintaining and extending them in the proper spirit, therefore also the trusteeship of the School, to which I should merely have furnished the [first ?] teachers, to be replaced from time to time.

R. W.

12. *Sep.* '77.

With this School, as will be understood, Wagner associated no pedagogic aim, in the manner of our Conservatoria (as to which he used to ask : " And *what* do they conserve ? ") : no, he expected sufficiently - trained *artistic individuals* to present themselves, for him to initiate into the special style of his works.   The opposition on every hand, however, was still so great and powerful, that Ferdinand Jäger *alone* had courage to announce himself.

When Wagner founded the " Bayreuther Blätter," and committed its control to Hans von Wolzogen, he purposely designed it, not for wide publicity, but simply for the circle of his friends.   To them alone were theoretic expositions of his artistic aims to be thus addressed.   The bond which united the friends of his art should "be kept alive and strengthened in the most instructive fashion."

*   *

*

In the summer of 1877 I had accepted the Presidentship of the Mannheim Court-theatre Committee, with the firm intention of transforming that institute in a Wagnerian sense. The brilliant traditions of the Mannheim stage, the independence of its administrators, and the circumstance that the performances could be thoroughly prepared, since— contrary to the custom of great cities—the theatre was opened but four times a week : all this made me approach my task with eagerness and the best of hopes.

Anton Seidl, who had acted as musical assistant at Bayreuth conjointly with Franz Fischer, applied for the soon vacant post of Kapellmeister, but withdrew his application upon reflecting that he had not yet had experience enough.

Dear Friend,

       Seidl informs me that he is renouncing his candidature for Mannheim.

He does well, and removes a stone from my heart, for— although gifted, he has no experience at all.—

All the more strongly do I commend *Fischer* to you. After I had been promised that he should be made a Musikdirektor, he has merely been given a place as choruspractiser (*Chorrepetitor*) ; which has offended me ! Fischer is thoroughly experienced, well up in the repertory, and an

out and out reliable man.   I answer for him !—Please tell
him of this my recommendation, and—procure him the
musical conductor's post to be shared with Langer.

His full name is : *Franz Fischer;* his exact address I
do not know ; but Hôtel *Vier Jahreszeiten* (his relations)
will see to it.

Best and heartiest greetings from

Yours

sincerely

RICHARD WAGNER.

BAYREUTH, 1. *Oct.* '77.

Meanwhile Hans Richter had taken into consideration my offer that he should assume the post of
Kapellmeister to the Mannheim theatre, as it would
allow of artistic work unhampered by the drawbacks
of great cities.   Upon my informing him of this,
Wagner telegraphed me :

*Richter ?   Good !   However, get Fischer good offer.   I
guarantee him.*

Parsifal.

I visited Wagner soon afterwards at Bayreuth.
With reference to the muddle prevailing on most
stages, he expressly recommended me to insist on
retaining the full right and power to cancel a
performance, even after the dress-rehearsal, if I did
not consider it sufficiently prepared.

As Richter remained in Vienna, Fischer was
appointed, and, after various preliminaries and
changes, I was able to apply to Wagner for the
right of performing the *Ring des Nibelungen.*   He
answered :

Most honoured Friend!

In reply to the question which you, as President of the Committee of the Grand-ducal Court-theatre at Mannheim, have most politely addressed to me regarding the acquisition of the right of performing all the parts of my Bühnenfestspiel "Der Ring des Nibelungen," I take leave to quote you the conditions under which I assign that right both now and in the future.

1. Production of the single parts in their proper order of succession. (Leipzig and Brunswick begin with "Rhein-gold" and "Walküre" on two successive evenings.)

2. Ten per cent of the gross receipts (including the quota of the abonnement) on every evening of performance of one of the pieces, down to expiry of the author's copy-right, i.e. 30 years after my death.

3. Guarantee that all the parts shall follow in due order : namely an advance of 10,000 marks, to be gradually re-funded by the half of every tantième, i.e. 5% of all receipts. As to one half, this advance is to be paid me in the sum of 5000 marks at the exchange of signatures, as to the other half, by a like sum of 5000 marks on the 1st of January next year, 1879.

These are the same conditions under which I have accorded the Leipzig Town-theatre the performing-right in question, whereas Hamburg has had to pay an advance of 16,000 marks—Vienna of 20,000 marks.

With the greatest friendship and respect,

Yours

faithfully

RICHARD WAGNER.

BAYREUTH, 14. *March*, 1878.

P.S. I have to remark, in your advantage, that the Mannheim Court-theatre will probably be the only theatre —at least as regards the Lower Rhine—that can offer performances of my work to the neighbouring population.

R. W.

By fulfilling these conditions I should have exceeded my powers, as I had to abide by the yearly Budget decreed by the Town-committee, and could not anticipate income by a grant of the wished-for advance.   The correspondence on this subject led to a few misunderstandings, which did not prevent Wagner, however, from giving me a personal proof of his unbounded confidence.

Dear Friend Heckel,
    I hereby give to *you*, for so long as you are in the unhappy position of a President of the Grand-ducal Theatre-committee at Mannheim, the right to perform every portion of my " Ring des Nibelungen " as often as you like and *for nothing*.—
    To the Mannheim theatre, which stands on a certain list of mine,[1] I will not bate a farthing.—
            This is the full earnest
                of your
                    old friend
                        RICHARD WAGNER.
BAYREUTH, 17. *March* 1878.

As I was not Director of the Mannheim theatre, but in my capacity of honorary President of its Committee had simply to consult the interests of the theatre, and not my own, the question was disposed of neither by the above nor by the following letter :

[1] A number of theatres, among them the Mannheim Court-theatre, paid Wagner no royalties on his earlier works, as they had entered into no binding contract at the time of purchase.   Only in later years was an arrangement with these theatres arrived at, whereby they agreed to pay royalties for *all* the works.

To Emil Heckel

113

Best Friend,

You are in error. At no time, nor at Heidelberg
either, have I *rejoiced* at your decision to accept the
presidentship of the Mannheim Theatre-committee; and
those present of my family very distinctly remember that
the words you quote as mine were used by Hotel-keeper
Albert, not by myself. However, as I saw that your
local triumph flattered you, I ended by rejoicing at this
triumph purely for yourself. On the contrary, I had to
regret that you paid so little heed to my serious scruples—
which I expressed to Zeroni also in particular. I simply
remember having said that, if anyone chose *me*, I shouldn't
know how to begin managing a theatre—especially if it
fell to me for reason of a heavy deficit—with any skill.
Only, you had confidence in yourself—and—so I held
silence.—

This is the truth, as concerns the one point.—

The other refers to the acquisition of the right of
performing my Nibelungen. You ask me a question
"as President of the Grand-ducal Theatre-committee." I
placed my requirements before you as such. You there-
upon informed my wife that the Mannheim Town-council
would expel you if you did but tell it my requirements.—
Candidly speaking, dear Heckel, *I* should have let myself
be expelled with pleasure. To be sure, the matter wears
a different look to you. Your position appeared to me
—excuse me!—unenviable. But if you believe that the
acquiring of the Nibelungen is an absolute necessity
of your staying on (at anyrate a great honour to me!),
I gladly offer it up to *your personal* continuance in
your position, so long as you deem the latter worth
maintaining.

So I renew my last offer to you: do with my Nibelungen
scores at Mannheim what *you* please; give concerts or
stage-performances. But only yourself, so long as you are
in it. May this declaration fortify you in making your

I

disclosures to the Mannheim magistrates without alarm.
I decline any bargaining !—
God keep you, dear old friend !
Your ever
devoted
RICHARD WAGNER.

BAYREUTH, 21. *March*, 1878.

And now—*not another word about this matter ! !*

I therefore made a personal journey to Bayreuth,
and very soon effected an agreement, as I had convinced myself of the impermissibility of my original
scheme, to follow the example of Schwerin and give
Die Walküre first, whilst Wagner met me in his
turn on every point that involved no abandonment of
artistic principles.

In Fritz Brandt we were fortunate enough to win
a quite exceptional capacity for our technical equip-
ment ; and as Hofrath Werther also, in his position
of Chief Regisseur, brought alike intelligence and
cordial interest to the work, the Mannheim preparations soon progressed apace.

In name of the Theatre-Committee I invited
Wagner to attend the performances.　He answered :

My most esteemed old Friend,
How could you delight me more, than by the good
news of the admirable progress of preparations for the
Mannheim performances of the Nibelungenring ? If one looks
closer into this state of things, it almost seems a wonder !
Fate has taken *its own* ways with my work : as they are
not the ways I had originally in view, it behoves me to
stand quietly and abstinently by, waiting for what may become

of the thing in this fashion.   That, then, is my present standpoint : I look on from a distance, rejoice at good results, and am not surprised by bad ones.   But—nowhere can I mix with them.   If you ever hear that I have any- where attended the performance of a portion of that work, you may accuse me of a breach of friendship : to that it will never come !—

So my heartiest thanks for the friendly invitation to Mannheim, which I beg you also to convey to the estimable gentlemen of the Grand-ducal Theatre-committee.

Full of the most grateful memories, I am ever mindful of your fervid zeal for my work and its execution, and remain

Your
most faithfully devoted
RICHARD WAGNER.

BAYREUTH, 23. *March* 1879.

The first Mannheim performances of *Das Rheingold* and *Die Walküre* took place at Easter, 1879 ; contrary to most other stages, without any cuts whatsoever, and exclusively with *our own* artists,— among whom Plank as "Wotan" laid the foundation of his artistic fame.   The success was altogether extraordinary.   I had begged Wagner "to be with me in thought, as I with him."   He sent me two telegraphic greetings, followed by a letter of the heartiest acknowledgment :

Congratulations and hearty greetings to all friends and comrades of the Mannheim Nibelungen-days !
Richard Wagner.

Thus virtue is rewarded.   Heckel forward !   Fischer

hurrah!   What would one more?   O Albert!   Heartily delighted,

Your   **R. W.**

My dear friend Heckel,

At last I get a moment to express to you my congratulations on your splendid achievements, also my own heartfelt delight at the success of your performances.   Until now, I have not been able to tear myself from my last labour at the composition of Parsifal: that now is finished, and you are the first to whom I turn myself outside again.

In your Mannheim there, you have set a most instructive example of what a valiant Will can do.   Since I have had to forgo a repetition of the performances at Bayreuth, nothing out the most careful reproduction on our usual public stages could shew at least what vitality there may be in my work—unless both it and its mission were to be entirely lost and forgotten.   That you went with trembling to your freely chosen task, upon comparing the means of your theatre with those of the very largest Upper-Court-stages, confirmed you in your resolution to advance according to my maxim namely to take the matter by its spirit: a thoroughly initiated, moreover a capable, energetic, and—above all—a convinced Conductor, such a one is pledge to me of everything.   Much as I have been delighted by the praise bestowed on Fischer, it hasn't in the least astonished me: I *knew* what he would do.   It really has been a great happiness to me, that, after having gained myself a few intelligent and good conductors, at last I have found a Theatre-director to summon one of them to office.   Hitherto my recommendations have always been injurious to the recommended: to our Messrs. Upper-Court Intendants, etc., nothing is more hateful than a so-called "Wagnerian," and their cry is: "Heaven help me!   I'm to be saddled with a man who wants a mass of rehearsals, especially when things go wrong ; and a man who won't cut out a note, notwithstanding that it all looks so much better when nicely unintelligible? No, no! I get on best with servile bunglers." Well, this time things were better in Mannheim; I hope it will also do good to future Leipzig performances, that the directorate there has willingly appointed a nominee of mine,[1] Fischer's companion at the Bayreuth performances.—And then our young Brandt! There there was something to be hoped, and the presumption that at last the whole management, to which I also owe my thanks, would be swept on to the right and proper. In such circumstances both performers and bandsmen work wonders. I have experienced it. But—the chief wonder remains—Heckel as Theatre-director! Good luck! Now I understand Fate, and greet you—in its shelter—from my whole heart!

Your trusty
RICHARD WAGNER.

BAYREUTH, 28. *April* 1879.

At the beginning of May I was able to inform Wagner that the third performance had gone off particularly well, and the Grand Duke of Baden had commanded me to sit beside him for its whole duration. I also related to the master the following little episode :—

At the entrance to the theatre I was saluted by a peasant from the Pfalz, who called to a little boy with flowers: "See, there's Herr Wagner. Give your godfather the posy." After I had corrected the man's mistake, he made the child speak out its name : "Richard Wagner." He then told me that the composer had consented to be its godfather, and they had come here on purpose to greet him. I gave

---

[1] Anton Seidl, engaged by Angelo Neumann.—TR.

father and son free tickets, and twitted the master on a certain Richard Wagner's having been at the performance after all.

From various quarters he had good accounts of the Mannheim performances, and Feustel wrote me : "Wagner is extremely contented with Mannheim." He therefore held out to Fischer, at a personal interview, the prospect of his still coming to one of the next performances, but wrote me soon thereafter :

Dearest Friend,

It grows more and more doubtful whether I shall be able to come to you at the end of this month ; that is precisely the time for which all our visitors—for instance, Liszt—have announced themselves this year ; also I am at the commencement of a course of waters, which may be very prolonged as the weather at present is not at all favourable.   I don't suppose I shall be able to leave here before the middle of August, and then propose to stop away till about the re-opening of your performances—somewhere in Switzerland, whence I *then* would come to you. It would be well if so much about this sort of thing didn't find its way into the papers at once !

I abide by it, that the success of your undertaking at Mannheim gives me quite peculiar joy.   Be assured of that !

Just now I feel very worn, and need great indulgence. But have no doubt of me, and remain always good to

Your

old good

RICHARD WAGNER.

BAYREUTH, 3. *July* 1879.

P.S. On his visit (to me most enjoyable) Fischer said

To Emil Heckel 119

something from you about the tantième payments. I leave it to you, to pay me the provisional 5 per cent at once or not. However—if you can, it would suit me if you *now* sent their amount to the end of *June* (1st half year)—I have some heavy disbursements!— R. W.

In August I attended performances of *Siegfried* and *Götterdämmerung* at Munich, which, together with much of excellence in the rendering, were marked by many operatic solecisms. I acquainted Wagner with my impressions in detail.

Dear Friend and Comrade,

If you have any money for me, you will do me a kindness by sending it. The 3rd quarter is always bad for a composer!

Your letter about the Munich performances went to my heart: I have told my King a deal about it, also about yourself!—

Now may all-kind Heaven shed its blessing on all further efforts! Frau Heckel and the Fischery—together with yourself—are heartily greeted by

Your
quite especially devoted
RICH. WAGNER.

BAYREUTH (*nowhere else!*) 17. Oct. '79.

The tantièmes at the Mannheim theatre were always paid for several performances in a lump; this led to Wagner's inquiries in the next:

Dear old Friend,

You surely must again have amassed some money for me of late; I'm not quite sure if I have already written begging you to have the *money* sent to Feustel at Bayreuth, the receipt-forms for my signature, however, to myself at "Villa Angri, Posilipo, Naples."

I hear nothing from you, not even—and unfortunately—
on the aforesaid business route. Am I already dead for all
Germania, then, or have you perished through theatric art?
For the rest, I am not being treated quite as I deserve:
we shall see if that will be improved by yourself.
Best greetings from villa to house! Remain good to
Your
thoroughly devoted
RICH. WAGNER.

NAPLES, 26. *March* 1880.

The early performances of *Rheingold* and *Walküre*,
which always drew a number of visitors from far and
wide, had given the Mannheim Court-theatre anew,
in the words of Richard Pohl, "an exceptional
renown." On the side of the Play they were matched
by unusual achievements, complete performances of
both parts of *Faust*, an *Iphigenia* trilogy (Euripides,
Sophocles, Goethe), two Shakespeare cycles (historical
dramas and comedies), and first productions of important new works. Now *Siegfried* and *Götterdämmerung* were to be mounted. This required a
larger outlay than the regular allowance of the town
provided for. As, however, when it came to passing
the Budget, the town refused to make any extra
grant, I resigned my post. Upon my informing
the master of this by letter, Frau Wagner sent me
his warmest compliments from Naples, and added:

You can look back on a chapter of your life with pride,
and return to your former sphere of action the richer by an
experience. In perhaps the most unfavourable circumstances
you have to record a sterling deed such as that of the Nibel-

To Emil Heckel

ungen-performances, fulfilled in the very brief period of your
tenure of office; and you have helped an excellent man, like
Fischer, not only to an appointment, but, what is of still
more importance, to the free development of his gifts. That
is much; and what is no less, is that you retire at the instant
when the narrow-heartedness of short-sighted men prevents
your being of further service to Art. That is worthy and
right; and if three years ago we could recognise in your
election a victory for our cause, in your withdrawal now
we greet a victory of yourself over all the fallacies which
others would assuredly have held before their eyes to keep
them to the post.

On the occasion of a meeting of Patrons at
Wiesbaden an " Executive Committee " (Friedrich
Schön, Emil Heckel, Richard Pohl) had been formed,
its main object being to induce the German Princes
to assist the undertaking, and in any case to back
Wagner's own efforts by a petition to the King of
Bavaria. To Schön, as chairman of this committee,
the master addressed a letter from Naples on June
28, 1880, of which the following is an extract :

My most highly honoured Friend !
How very much I necessarily regret perceiving, from
your letter to my dear wife, that you have been placed in a
little uncertainty about me. I should be glad to know, if
you would lay a scheme before me, what is the precise
authorisation you require from me for an agitation in favour
of the Bayreuth idea, in order that I might grant your wish
at once. Only, as regards the plan of execution I beg you
to set a little store by my experience, concerning alike the
German world and myself. Thus I could wish that you
would no longer thrust my draft of September 1877 too

much into the foreground, as all my experience reaped since then has shewn me that at that time—I admit, not quite unconsciously—I made my reckoning without the host.   On the other hand, if I review the hopes aroused in me and all our friends since your own intervention, I can see no other possibility of meeting your wishes at last, than that I should attempt to revive the interest not yet woken since the Festivals of 1876—as you opine—by a performance of "Parsifal" to be effected as soon as possible.   To me this project seems executable in the year 1882, if only I can be left in absolute peace; but that itself—as regards the outward possibility—only if I claim the aid of the King of Bavaria for it. — — —

In circumstances thus assured, after "Parsifal" I think of presenting to my friends one of my older works each year—thus eventually all in series—in model performances, as my artistic testament.   As I now am in my 68th year, for the execution of this plan I have to count upon a high and vigorous old age; and therewith I fancy I shall have done enough, consequently that I may be exempted from the performances of "Zauberflöte," "Freischütz," "Fidelio" and so on.   Whatever I can teach and impart in that respect, I will gladly do in private,—one only needs to visit me at Bayreuth. If with those performances of my own works I do not leave my "school" behind me, I can have nothing whatever to do with a "school." — — —

King Ludwig accorded that the orchestra of the Munich Court-theatre, under Kapellmeister Hermann Levi, should be placed at Wagner's disposal at Bayreuth during two whole summer-months, for the performance of *Parsifal*.

In November, 1880, with Richard Pohl I welcomed the master on his return from Italy—at Munich, where Lenbach and Gedon had prepared a grand festivity in his honour. Pohl and I had gone to Munich, as members of the Executive Committee, to consult with Wagner about immediate measures. After this conference the performances were definitely announced for 1882, in Wagner's "Communication to the honoured Patrons of the Stage-festivals at Bayreuth"[1]; the number of Patrons, however, was too small for the festivals to be got up for them alone, according to his original intention, and the "public" was therefore to be admitted once again.

In January another meeting at Bayreuth became requisite. Wagner wished the sinking-fund amassed by the Patronatverein (the so-called "eiserner Fond") to be drawn upon if necessary; this the Verwaltungs-rath deemed unallowable, and I therefore told him that we probably should meet with difficulties in such a course. The master sprang to his feet, and for once I myself had to weather a "storm" such as I had several times been witness of, particularly before the earlier festivals.

It was thoroughly in keeping with the master's recklessly open nature and admirable truthfulness, that he should give free rein to his excitement and anger at crucial moments; then all the pent-up wrath and sorrow of former experiences would explode with elemental force. Thus I remember his bursting out at a clumsy remark about his reading of Beethoven's Ninth Symphony, until the victim sank back weeping on his chair. To be sure, Wagner then went up

[1] See *Prose Works*, vi. 36.—Tr.

to him, and offered him his hand : "Don't make
such remarks again : and now not another serious
word."—"*And now not another serious word!*"
How often have I heard that sentence from his lips.
He would calm himself with it after heated alterca-
tions, or quell any tendency to gush after harrowing
artistic impressions, and cut the topic short.   In
general, he didn't like to have all the talk to himself,
and often would end a lengthy speech with the sudden
interjection : "No, I've been talking long enough ;
it's your turn now."—Yet another violent outburst
of Wagner's still clings to my memory.   Through
preference given to other parties, the execution of
certain orders for the Festspielhaus had been postponed beyond the stipulated term, causing a perilous
delay : his whole disgust at the disrespect so often
shewn to German Art out of servile considerations,
or for sake of faddish amateurs, then came to an
explosion.   Yet neither in this case did he bear the
smallest grudge against the delinquent, who stood as
if paralysed by Wagner's energy.

Remembering such experiences, it boded no good
to me when I saw Wagner leap up, after my remark
about employment of the sinking-fund. He shouted :
"What!   Heckel, you can speak of 'difficulties'?
You're the very last person I should have expected
it from!"   He rang off all the obstacles that had
already been thrown in the path of himself and his
enterprise, looked straight at me, and said : "How
can *you*, of all people, revive these memories in me
by that abominable word?"   I tried to pacify him :

in vain. Every unpleasantness that had ever happened
to him in a similar way, came back to his mind, and
he hurled them all at me in towering passion. Many
of the items I myself had gone through with him,
but others were new to me and held my whole
attention. Suddenly he came to a pause: "Why!
all the time I've been flurrying myself, he (pointing
to me) has been sitting coolly there, just listening to
a story." Turning to the painter Joukowsky, he
added already half-humorously: "You see how he
treats me."

No lasting disagreement ever came between us.
I, too, could always allow myself a candid and out-
spoken expression of my mind. To be sure, I had
no great learning to back me, but I ventured to pass
for what I am, trusting to my instinctive feeling;
and whoever placed himself in the service of Wagner's
genius for attainment of its artistic ends, consequently
in the service of Art itself, without therefore discard-
ing his own independence, was assured of the master's
heartiest acknowledgment and gratitude. For that
matter, Richard Wagner had a rooted dislike of
people who knew just enough to prate of culture,
without possessing any power of self-improvement;
on the other hand, he valued all immediate sensibility.
Once, upon my telling him of my intention to find
another adit to his works through the study of
Schopenhauer, he laughed outright, saying: "Heckel,
why don't you stick to your own common-sense?"

*   *

*

After the meeting of January 1881 I left Bayreuth in a highly satisfied humour, and wrote Wagner about my confidence in the success of the coming festivals.

Through the instrumentality of Hans von Wolzogen, the master was given a birthday surprise by his wife, who had had his library ceiling decorated with the arms of all the cities where Wagner-Vereins had proved their zeal for his undertaking.

At a Bayreuth conference in July 1881 it was resolved, on my proposal, to get *guarantees* signed in provision against a deficit. I was soon enabled to send good news from Mannheim about this; also about my negotiations with Messrs. Schott's Sons, of Mainz, concerning the publication of *Parsifal*.

Since I had received no letter in the master's own handwriting for some while, I pointed this out to him, but without intending any reproach. At like time I transmitted him an arithmetical calculation of the bars in his various works. The computer wished these toilsome tables to be published in the *Bayreuther Blätter*, which then were sent to every Patron. How little favour the master shewed such curiosa, in which Wagnerian "literature" perhaps is over-rich, is proved by his half-humorous half-testy answer :

Oh ! old Friend !
    Must you, too, make life hard to me by seeing a slight in my getting my wife to answer an inquiry of yours, when it has to be done at the very time that I am sitting at my score ?

There seem to be idlers who can always write letters !—perhaps it happens to myself at times.—

Dearest—the enclosure I return to you—with 1000 thanks (of course). I cannot possibly present myself before our Patrons with such facetiæ !

Much thanks for all friendship !
Always your
old
RICH. WAGNER.

BAYREUTH, 2. *July* 1881.

After terminating his Mannheim contract, Franz Fischer had found an honourable sphere of work as Kapellmeister to the Munich Court ; Fritz Brandt, after the death of his father, was summoned to *Bayreuth* by the following letter of the master's :

Dear valued young Friend !

Thanks for your letter,—it was beautiful ! Only to-day do I write you, as this mournful business had to be postponed because my health is such that my dear wife was afraid even to impart to me the news of the so terribly sudden death of your beloved father at the time : an accident revealed to me this stroke of Fate !—

I am sure you will understand me, and forgive me, if I do not frame my feelings in words. I am in the third age of man's life, and already have seen two generations of contemporaries pass away : in your father I have lost the last member of that second group which still linked me to the past. In yourself I salute the third generation, to which I have to commit my ripe life for continuing. Be you welcome ! I assume that you are ready to carry out the last act of your father's joint work with me.

At anyrate everything for it stands at your disposal, and you know exactly what is involved in the scenic representation of Parsifal.

Permit me therefore to summon you to fill your lamented father's place in my Bayreuth performances.   In my absence from Bayreuth, for a few months yet, my Verwaltungsrath will gladly assist you with every information and requisite arrangement.   Please order whatever you consider needful.

To the most sincere condolence with your cherished lady mother I add the assurance of the friendliest attachment to yourself of

Your

deeply sorrowing

RICHARD WAGNER.

PALERMO, HÔTEL DES PALMES, 14. *January* 1882.

Frau Wagner acquainted me by letter with the progress in the orchestration of *Parsifal.*   She was always wrapt up in Wagner's work, and just as with the *Ring des Nibelungen* before, she took her full share in the preparations for presenting *Parsifal.* Wagner often boasted of the extraordinary help she had been to him.   Thus I remember the moment when the first pianoforte stage–rehearsal was about to commence : Wagner stepped up to his wife, almost ceremoniously, with the words : " Come wife, you have helped me to create my work ; now take your place beside me ! "—then, turning to me : " Come Heckel, too ! "   We took our station on the stage among the artists unoccupied in this rehearsal.

It was an invariable rule at Bayreuth, that all performers engaged for one and the same rôle should attend its each rehearsal, to lay to heart the master's remarks to the others about its conception and execution. This engendered a healthy emulation between the several performers to gain an insight into the master's intentions, and, applying it to the free unfolding of their natural idiosyncrasy, to outstrip each other in those points where either's individuality supplied advantage. Owing to this rivalry among the impersonators of the rôle of Kundry, for instance, Frau Materna and Fräulein Brandt brought out the best the elemental savagery of the first act, whilst Fräulein Malten's wheedling temptress in the second act, and humble penitent in the third, will perhaps be never equalled.

Just as the matchless combination of the voices of the three Rhine-daughters formed a special joy to Wagner in 1876, in 1882 he was particularly delighted with the scene of the "Flower-fays," prepared by "Blumenvater" Porges. After its last rehearsal he told me, with an expression of the utmost happiness and satisfaction : "That's the *first* time I've seen and heard a scene upon the stage exactly as I *conceived* it. Heckel, it's wonderful!"

Of all the performers, it was Scaria who brought the highest individuality to his task ; Wagner therefore allowed him a perfectly free hand in the moulding of "Gurnemanz."

During the main rehearsals for the *Ring des Nibelungen* Wagner sat as a rule at a little table on the stage, as shewn in a delicious caricature of Menzel's. For the rehearsals of *Parsifal*, on the contrary, he was mostly seated in the front row of the auditorium. He had a little window made in

the hood above the orchestra, to enable him to speak
to the conductor.

The business side of the rehearsals and performances was committed to Adolph Gross and myself,
to whom executants alike and visitors were referred
by a placard on the Festspielhaus.   By desire of the
King of Bavaria a special portico was added to the
front, to give the King a separate entrance.   Nevertheless, he did not attend the *Parsifal* performances
at Bayreuth, but had it repeated for himself thereafter, by the same artists, at a private representation
in Munich.

The first two performances of *Parsifal*, on the
26th and 28th July 1882, were reserved for the
members of the Patronatverein, to whom the master
thus fulfilled his obligations.   He saw himself compelled to dissolve the Verein, as certain busybodies
had misconstrued their function and wished to impose their ideas on the management.

The penultimate performance was attended by the
German Crown-Prince (subsequently Kaiser Friedrich III.).   After the first act, he said to me : " I
can find no words for the impression I have just
received ; it surpasses everything I had expected ; it
is stupendous ; I am deeply moved, and comprehend
that this work can never form part of our modern
repertoire."   When Burgomaster Muncker and
Banker Feustel came into the antechamber of his
box, after the representation was over, he told them :
" Herr Heckel has been witness of my enthusiasm ;
I can only express my admiration once again.   I feel

as if I were not in a theatre, so sublime is it all."
Four years later, he again attended a performance of
Parsifal at Bayreuth.

Most of the royal personages who visited Bayreuth preferred to travel incognito. Thus it happened that in 1876 the Emperor of Brazil, wishing
to enter the Festspielhaus before the time, was turned
away by the attendants, until I heard of it and gave
him entry.

The rehearsals and performances of *Parsifal*
were marked by fewer froward incidents than the
"Nibelungen-days." This may have been due, in
part to the nature of the work itself, in part to better
regulation.

At the end Wagner gave us a grand surprise, an
experience I shall never forget. Before the last
performance he unexpectedly resolved to conduct the
last act of his Bühnenweihfestspiel himself, from the
changing scene onwards. His intention was made
known to few. Levi and Fischer, the regular conductors of *Parsifal*, remained in the orchestra, so
that the executants might not miss their accustomed
cues at certain passages. The master was therefore
able to devote himself exclusively to a thoroughly
adequate rendering of rhythm and expression. It
was marvellous, the profound feeling and mighty
breadth conferred on the drawn-out phrases. The
puissance of the great scene for Amfortas exceeded
anything I have ever witnessed ; Reichmann, its
exponent, told me after the performance : "A thing
like that, one can only go through once. To such

an expenditure of breath, such a tax on one's strength of voice in general, only the master himself can pin one." The wind-players in the orchestra said much the same. Every executant had willingly put forth his utmost power. What that hour revealed to us, came never back. The conducting of the last act of *Parsifal* was Wagner's last act as conductor. Hardly anybody in the audience knew that the master himself was wielding the bâton, nor was it known to many after.

The financial results of 1882 surpassed our expectations. Neither the guarantee, nor the " eiserner Fond," was drawn upon ; and now the latter could really form a sinking-fund for future performances.

At my request Frau Wagner sent me a photograph of the master, after the festival :

" Adolf Gross tells me that you would like to have a photograph of my husband, and that a signed one. Here it follows with a smile from my husband, as he knows how many of his letters you possess, and evidences of his friendliest esteem. — — — What a friend you have proved yourself again ! And how our ' system ' has been justified of its result ! Accept our thanks and greetings, in most cordial and unalterable friendship to you and your dear ones, from all at Wahnfried."

At Bayreuth, during the *Parsifal* performances, I had received the news of my re-election to the Mannheim Theatre-Committee. One merry night at Wahnfried the master asked me : " And what great things do the Mannheimer expect from you, then ? "

To Emil Heckel   133

"That I shall bring *Parsifal* in my pocket," was my answer, "nothing less could induce them." This tickled Wagner immensely, and I had to tell him much besides about my native city.

I was little disposed, after enjoyment of the Bayreuth Festspiel, to devote myself once more to the everyday business of a theatre; but there still remained much to be done in this way for the cause. That decided me; and by the autumn of 1882 I therefore was able to write Wagner, then at Venice, that I had taken up my election as President of the Theatre-Committee. Soon afterwards, when sending Frau Wagner a photograph of my family, I had the pleasure of giving her good accounts of the theatre, and telling her that a star-engagement of Fräulein Malten (the Bayreuth "Kundry") had made me dream of a "Lohengrin-performance" at Mannheim, with Fräulein Malten as Elsa, and under the master's own direction. Frau Wagner's reply held out a possibility of the dream's being fulfilled:

"What a beautiful dream! It certainly means something, and who knows whether it will not yet be fulfilled! The verdict on Fräulein Malten particularly pleased my husband; he has a great opinion of her. So your kind letter was full of good, which we reciprocate with all our hearts."

Concerning a performance of the whole first act of *Parsifal*, to be given in the *concert-room* at Mannheim, I received the following telegram:

Whole first act too much and wearisome; finale, from changing scenery onwards, would suffice.

Wagner.

A second telegram accidentally arrived open at the theatre-bureau. Wagner wrote me with regard to it :

Dear Friend,
        Thanks, congratulations—for past and future ; also my humble compliments to the discreet telegraph-officials at Mannheim.—

And now :—after all, my wife has forgotten to tell you what I now retrieve :—do engage the Augsburg Frank for your theatre ; I guarantee him, and consider him excellent in every respect. You already will know how to pass him in ; if at the time of your former exit they gave you a reactionary as schoolmaster, and Fischer therefore had to go, things now might happen *vice versâ*.

As you have seen, other powers don't stick at trifles !—

Think it over, and be assured—etc.

Gross was here yesterday : this time we are only to have July, and 12 performances. Well, well ! I fret myself at nothing more, and now shall let myself be massé twice a day !

The like is wished you by
Your
very trusty
RICH. WAGNER.

VENICE, 14. *Jan.* 1883.

Wagner had intended *twenty-four* performances of *Parsifal* for 1883 ; this will explain the humorous words at the close, over which I heartily laughed. Entering into the joke, I replied that if it would be of any service to him, I would willingly get myself massaged four times daily. Little did I dream that these were the last letters ever to pass between us.

As late as February 10—three days before her husband's death—Fráu Wagner wrote me without any apprehension of a crisis. I had expressed a hope that the master would return through the Gothard, so as to visit me at Mannheim. It fell out otherwise. His homeward road was taken, as a corpse, over the Brenner again to his beloved German Bayreuth.

— — —

If I abstained from depicting the profound impressions made upon me by the Festspiels, with still more justice may I withhold my feelings at the news of the great master's death, my sensations at his solemn burial in Bayreuth. Here, as so often in life, applies that deeply earnest word from the first act of *Parsifal* :—

" That ne'er is told."—

*   *

*

Frau Wagner's condition remained so precarious for a long time after the master's death, that it was impossible for her to take any personal part in the festival of 1883. The sense of mourning was universal. How quiet every movement on the stage, what an earnest hush among the audience when it took its customary promenade before the playhouse in the entr'actes. The thought of the departed master was manifest on every face.

Scaria undertook the stage-management. Every effort was directed to preserving the master's intentions down to the smallest detail. Remarks and observations of witnesses of the 1882 and 1883 performances, alike executants and spectators, were collected in a volume to be kept at Wahnfried. Forty pages here record those notes on the master's own rendering, and subsequent deviations, all tabulated under act and person. This chronicle has proved of the greatest service for retention of the original character of the performances.

The Verwaltungsrath, reinforced by Friedrich Schön as administrator of the " Richard Wagner Stipendiary-fund," had taken over the business department as in previous Festspiel years. In place of Frau Wagner, the children of the " villa Wahnfried " sent a letter of thanks to the Verwaltungsrath :

"We know very well that the self-sacrificing energy you have devoted to our father's cause again this year springs from an enthusiasm which bears its happiness in itself, and no expression of thanks can ever recompense. Yet we feel it a debt to ourselves, to tell you how deeply and sincerely we recognise that the profoundest sentiments have inspired you once again successfully to speed our father's work. It is Love that you have proved us ; love it is, that we return you ; and heartily we beg you, of your kindness to accept its deeply-moved expression."

Repetitions of the " Parsifal-performances " could be announced for 1884. On a visit to Mannheim, Adolf Gross informed me that Frau Wagner still was keeping the strictest seclusion, and wished to have no personal hand in these coming Festspiels either, but intended begging me to convey her messages to the artists during the rehearsals and representations. Subsequently Frau Wagner determined to attend at least the preparations, behind the scenes, and communicate with the Regisseur direct.

*   *
*

Immediately after Wagner's death I organised a solemn celebration at the Mannheim Court-theatre (with poem by Karl Heckel), repeated at Bremen later.

The Mannheim representations of *Siegfried* and *Götterdämmerung* were highly successful. On the occasion of the first performances of the latter work I had the honour of welcoming Liszt and his grandchildren to my house. Other persons concerned with the Bayreuth undertaking also came to the Mannheim performances. Frau Wagner wrote me :—

"Siegfried gives me such glowing accounts of the performances of ' Götterdämmerung,' that I cannot refrain from expressing to you how much I am touched by what you have accomplished."

At Frau Wagner's instigation I begged Court-operasinger Knapp, who had proved an unexceptionable Gunther, to study the part of Amfortas with Kapellmeister Seidl, for singing at Bayreuth. Unfortunately, again he never arrived at a final consent.

As my house was being rebuilt, I gave Johannes Hoffart of Charlottenburg (at that time of Munich) —a sculptor whose sturdily German style had won my particular sympathy—the order for a colossal bust of Wagner in carrara marble. Frau Wagner had the kindness to advise me in approval of the sketch ; by her recommendation all symbols of the antique world, such as laurel and lyre, were omitted.

Reporting to Wahnfried a complete cycle of the *Ring des Nibelungen*, I closed my letter with the words : "Only the erection of the bust upon my house and the production of *Tristan und Isolde* at our local Court-theatre, and my mission at Mannheim is at end." For the unveiling of the bust on September 15, 1887—the first public monument ever raised to Wagner—the artists of the Mannheim stage arranged a most successful ceremony. Commencing with the Kaisermarsch and the "Wacht auf" chorus from *Die Meistersinger*, rendered by members of the Court-theatre, it ended with an oration by Chief-Regisseur Martersteig. Various guests of honour and a close-packed public attended the ceremony. The building received the name of "Richard Wagner-house " : upon many an occasion thereafter its doors were opened to the master's family.

When *Tristan und Isolde* was about to be performed at Mannheim, Frau Wagner attended the rehearsals, and gave us many valuable hints in preparation of the work.

Besides Max Martersteig, who proved his practical ability and fine artistic taste as Oberregisseur, I had succeeded later in acquiring Felix Weingartner as Hofkapellmeister ; he gladly left the Hamburg Town-theatre, to find at Mannheim a free field for

his artistic energy. My hopes of getting him called
to Bayreuth, however, were not to be fulfilled.

In course of time the number and power of those
among the Mannheim audience, too, who seek diver-
sion instead of concentration at the theatre, increased
so greatly as to countervail our efforts for correct
performances in Wagner's spirit. True, Weingartner
and Martersteig stood loyally by my side against
inartistic demands, as for cuts, etc., which found
expression even in the Committee itself. "Cut *me*
out first!" was Weingartner's manly retort.
Certainly this foiled the contemplated mutilation of
Wagner's works, but vanity and pretentious dilettantism, notwithstanding, obtained the upper hand. I
could see no fruitful field of action before me any
longer, and so, after ten years' service, my duties at
the Mannheim Court-theatre ended, as said in the
letter above referred to, with the production of
Tristan und Isolde. Later on, I was re-elected to the
re-organised Management, but declined the office.

Frau Wagner wrote me :

"How one triumphs, and on what one founders, is the
main affair ; and so I picture you, dear friend, as contented
as any man may be who has done his best for a good cause,
and is therefore justified in hoping that that best will not be
lost."

*   *

*

Wagner had always cherished the intention of
calling quite a number of conductors to Bayreuth, to

teach them the great importance of the scenic picture and dramatic action, down to their tiniest details, to the Kapellmeister.   He was never tired of saying that an insight into the drama gave the proper tempo of itself.   It has therefore been the prime and constant aim of Bayreuth, to render justice to the drama.

With *Tristan und Isolde* in 1886, Frau Wagner shewed the world her extraordinary capacity for independent pursuance of the master's steps.   The great scene in the second act stood out most markedly from anything presented at the usual theatres : it was no longer taken as a " love-duet," and every receptive spectator must have had it borne-in on him that, in the stricter meaning of the word, this scene involves a dramatic progress—Tristan's accomplishing of life-denial in the heart of Isolde.[1]   Moreover, in Frau Sucher an artist had been found, for the first time perhaps, to present a fully adequate embodiment of " Isolde."

Tristan und Isolde, under Mottl, was the last work witnessed at Bayreuth by Wagner's noble friend, Franz Liszt.   His death in mid-festival fell upon many of us as a personal bereavement.

The next festival year [1888] brought *Die Meistersinger von Nürnberg*.   Just as I had been

---

[1] See Karl Heckel : *Erläuterungen zu " Tristan und Isolde."* [In an article on " The Tristan drama " in *The Meister* for Feb. 1893 I have taken the opposite view of this process, namely, that it is Isolde who leads Tristan imperceptibly along the chain that starts with the extinction of the torch and ends in that " sweet Death " she earlier had offered him.   Perhaps it is simply a question of temperament, whether one regards Tristan *or* Isolde as the chief character in the drama.—TR.]

privileged to greet the Kaisers Wilhelm I. and
Friedrich III. (then Crown-prince) at Bayreuth, I
now was gladdened by the warm interest shewn by
Kaiser Wilhelm II. After the performance he told
me that he had never known, till then, how much of
Die Meistersinger was cut at Berlin. In the result
the Berlin performances, too, were given without cuts.

Ensuing years, the years of *Tannhäuser*, *Lohengrin*,
and the revival of the *Ring des Nibelungen*, rejoiced
in a constantly increasing attendance, whilst larger
and larger circles were convinced of the Bayreuth
aim to attain a whole and grand impression through
the *harmony* of many units. What somewhat lacked
in these representations, however, was *individuality*
in the performers, an individuality *fully* covering the
task, such as had been displayed so lately as by Herr
Friedrichs in the part of " Beckmesser." It would
almost seem that, for all the energy which in-
dividualism now asserts in literature, our age has
fewer and fewer masterful personalities to shew
among its reproductive artists ; yet no imitative
execution of instructions, however faithful, can ever
supply the place of spontaneous conception.— — —

The performances of *Der Ring des Nibelungen* in
1896 constituted a celebration of the Festivals first
held just twenty years before. A quarter of a
century had flown, since the undertaking began to
gain firm ground through Wagner's Appeal to the
Friends of his art,[1] the Patronat-committee and the
founding of Wagnervereins. How slow had been

---

[1] See *Prose Works*, vol. v. p. 312 *et seq.*—Tr.

the march, 'spite every effort! To what attacks had Wagner's little band of comrades been exposed, when, like the admirable Privy Councillor von Muncker of Bayreuth, they courageously proclaimed their belief in the undertaking from the very first, and year by year evinced their practical devotion in countless struggles to reconcile conflicting interests!

A retrospect of that past quarter-of-a-century revives in me many valued memories, knit-up with all the personages who took immediate part in the adventure. The letters directed to me personally in the Bayreuth cause exceed the number of two thousand, among them over sixty from Wagner himself and countless other treasured documents from notabilities. I think with gratitude of all the fruits I owe to Wagner and his art.

Looking back on those five-and-twenty years gone by, I longed to give this sentiment a visible expression. The bâton wherewith the master had conducted the "Siegfried-Idyll" for the first time at Mannheim the 20th of December 1871, I sent to Frau Wagner at Bayreuth with these lines:—"Five and twenty years have flown since the master, by the trust and friendliness with which he greeted my first letter, conferred on me a task worth living for. Every backward glance on that glorious time is a feast to me. In memory of the earliest personal meeting, on the occasion of our Mannheim concert, I send you the bâton for Wahnfried."

Like everything else relating to the master, it there is most religiously preserved. Fräulein Eva

Wagner wrote me in acknowledgment : "I think the hallowing it once received must prosper here anew."

*   *

*

The more frequent repetition of the festivals in later years made it necessary to simplify the administration. To Herr Commerzienrath Adolf von Gross, as valued agent of the family and guardian of Siegfried Wagner, the business management has more and more exclusively passed, in place of the Verwaltungsrath.

I have never had anything to do with the conduct of the "Allgemeiner Richard Wagner-Verein," which sprang up after Wagner's death, yet hoped to see it carry out my project of a "German Wagnerverein." After repeated attempts by certain of its members to interfere in the administration itself, it has been energetically taught its place by Bayreuth. As the master was driven by force of circumstance to give the Festivals to unconditional publicity, and public they have remained, the financial intervention of a Verein was no longer requisite. On the other hand, by acting in due harmony with Bayreuth it might have attained to great importance as a sort of *national coadjutor*; for, as Wagner built his Festspielhaus at no cosmopolitan watering-place, but amid the quiet hush of Bayreuth, he hoped to gather there a yearly public to celebrate a *German* festival. Had he merely wished for stage-representations in a theatre built expressly for the purpose, he could have had his wish at any of several different places, as so many of his letters to me attest. For that he would have needed no Verwaltungsrath, no Patrons, no Vereins. But what Richard Wagner wanted, was community between Artist and Folk.

There remains another institution, *called into life by himself*, to which a kindred mission falls : the *Richard Wagner Stipendien-Stiftung*. As it is in constant receipt of help from Bayreuth, so it should receive much more generous aid from without. It was always one of Wagner's pet ideas, to distribute a large proportion of the places gratis, and to enable the less well-to-do to attend the festivals through a grant of travelling-expenses. The funds of this foundation are not yet large enough to carry out its noble task in full ; every contribution signifies a furtherance of the National idea knit-up by Wagner in the Festspiels. As to these national and cultural plans we are instructed in his *Gesammelte Schriften* [Prose Works] ; only by acquaintance therewith can the reader fully comprehend the master's aims and objects.

Of late years the son of Richard Wagner, Siegfried, has taken a more and more prominent part in the festivals, and with growing success. The future of Bayreuth, as a habitation consecrate to German Art, is bound up with his name. May our hopes of him be realised to the full !

On earlier pages I have repeatedly shewn how little the master was contented by the mere outward

prospering of an undertaking, nay, how it enraged
him to be congratulated on his "successes" when he
could nowhere find an understanding of his goals.
He would never allow that an artwork was actively
alive, so long as it was simply accepted as a sop from
its creator without any feeling of relationship between
Artist and Folk. It was the direct participation of
the Folk itself, its national interest in Art, that
Wagner sought before all else, and that made him
rate the labours of his friends far higher than ever
could be merited by their purely practical results.
Thus it was, he wrote me at that period when the
realisement of the Festivals was trembling in the
balance:

"*So we will hope, then! On the path you have
struck with such energy and prudence we yet may find
still-hidden forces of the German nature: this is of
almost greater importance than the success of the undertaking itself*" [Letter of Nov. 19, 1873].

And even though, taken as a whole, the public
hoped by Wagner has not been found, we must not
forget how many every year have grown aware
through "Bayreuth" of the earnest aims of his
German Art, and in how many its shining hill awakes
the love of genius.

"Ehrt eure deutschen Meister,
dann bannt ihr gute Geister!"

Index

As in my index to " Richard Wagner's Letters to Wesendonck," the figures denoting tens and hundreds are not *repeated* for one and the same reference, or sub-division of a reference. Footnotes are marked with an " *n* " after the numeral.—W. A. E.

"Mode, Was die," 36.

Money, 7, 54, 92, 8, 102, 11-2, 9. See Bayreuth.

Mottl, Felix, 140.

Mrazeck, Franz, 19, 26.

Muchanoff, M. von, 5, 16.

Mühldorfer, Jos., 44-5.

Müller, Frl. von, 73, 4, 6, 85.

Muncker, von, 31, 130, 42.

Munich, 9, 13, 9, 26, 58, 89, 110, 22 ; Court, 62, 70 ; Theatre, 2, 71, 8, 100, 19, 22, 7, 30—tantièmes, 104.

Music-shops, 53, 7, 60.

Musical societies, 2, 3, 22, 41, 3, 105.

Musik. Wochenblatt, 25, 7 *n.*, 33 *n.*, 89, 92.

"Musikdrama," 43.

N. K., 22.

Naples, 119, 21.

National undertaking, a, 4, 12, 21, 3, 25, 6, 36-8, 51, 3, 60, 4, 100, 4, 143-5.

Nature, gifts of, 72.

Neue deutsche Rundschau, v, 27 *n.*, 41 *n.*

Neuhofer, flautist, 43.

New Year's greeting, 72.

"Nibelungen-treasury," 90.

Nicknames, 24-5.

Niemann, Albert, 36, 7, 87.

Nietzsche, Elizabeth, 48, 57 *n.*

Nietzsche, Friedrich, 21, 3, 4, 7, 37, 8, 55, 9, 101 ; letter, 57.

Nohl, Ludwig, 23, 43.

Norns' scene, 44, 73.

"Not another word," 114, 24.

Oberon, 45.

Orchestra, 7, 9, 19, 20, see Bayreuth.

Owls and theatre, 61.

Palermo, H. des Palmes, 128.

Panic, financial, 60.

Parsifal: comp. finished, 116 ; orchestration, 126, 8 ; poem, reading, 105-6 ; publication, 126;—performances, 122, 123, 3, 7-32 ; W. conducting, 131-2, at Munich, 130 ; concert, 133.

Parson, the, 105.

Partenkirchen, 8.

Patroclus, 50.

Patrons, 32, 51-3, 65, 77, 8, 93, 4, 6, 98, 101, 4, 44 ; committee, 4, 5, 9, 10, 55-6, 121, 3, 41 ; Verein, 102-3, 106-8, 23, 6 — dissolved, 130 ; Vouchers, 4-7, 13, 29, 30, 41, 55, 68, 80, 3, 90, 104.

Pauer, Max, 55.

Pesth, 76, 7, 81.

Pfalz, peasant from, 117.

Photographs, 15, 6, 133, see W.

"Pickelhaube," 46.

Placards, 33, 94, 130.

Plank as Wotan, 115.

Pohl, R., 21, 3, 5, 105, 20, 1, 2, 3.

Polemics, vi, 22, 47, 88.

Politics, 66.

Porges, Heinrich, 26, 129.

Posilipo, 119.

Power and consciousness, 102.

Press, the, 10, 5, 8, 24, 36, 51-2, 8, 9, 64, 9, 100, 18.

Princes, 20, 65-6, 94, 121, 30-1.

Principle, 60, 114, 21.

Public, the, 11, 52, 4, 9, 68, 90, 100-103, 8, 23, 35, 41, 3, 5. See also Germans.

R., theatre-presid., 45.

Rehearsals, 110, 6 ; Bayreuth, 72-80, 85-90, 109, 17, 28-31, 6-7 ; dress, 91, 4 ; visitors at, 81 ; concert, 16-21, 77.

Reich, restored, 3, 62, 3, 6.

Reichenberg, von, 74, 8, 9.

Reichmann, Theodor, 131.

Reichstag, 64.

"Rheinfahrt, Siegfried's," 44.

Rheingold, Das, 78 ; score sent to Brahms, 84. See Loge, etc.

Rhine-daughters, 73, 129.

Richter, Hans, 2, 35, 40, 70, 2 *n.*, 103, 110 ; honeymoon, 76.

Riedel, Prof., 36.

Riehl, W. H., 33.

154 Letters of Richard Wagner

THE END

Printed by R. & R. Clark, Limited, *Edinburgh.*

Printed in the United States
By Bookmasters